To Natasha — noise about

**What every entrepreneur, fi
small business owner needs to know about Public Relations**

PR ON A BEERMAT

LOUISE THIRD

Printed in Great Britain
By Amazon

"There is only one thing in the world worse than being talked about, and that is not being talked about."

Oscar Wilde, The Picture of Dorian Gray (1890)

We dedicate this book to all those clients
who have trusted us to manage their reputation.

May you continue to be talked about.

© Louise Third 2021

Louise Third had asserted her right under the Copyright, Designs and Patents Acts, 1988, to be identified as the author of this work.

The information in this book has been compiled by way of general guidance in relation to the subjects addressed and is not intended as a substitute for specific professional advice. The authors and the publishers disclaim as far as the law allows any liability arising directly or indirectly from the use or misuse of any information contained in this book.

ISBN: 9798533860840

Cover design by Hallam

Fans of PR on a Beermat

"Quite possibly the clearest, most readable book ever explaining what PR is, and what PR isn't. I can't recommend it highly enough."

Francis Ingham MPRCA, Director General, Public Relations and Communications Association.

"Louise Third shows the variety of ways in which entrepreneurs can do their own PR with little or no financial outlay. She demonstrates that the opportunities are boundless. I will certainly use it in my Business Start Up class."

Professor Colin Mason, Adam Smith Business School, University of Glasgow.

"PR On a Beermat does a fantastic job of simplifying a challenging discipline! An essential guide for anyone looking to gain an understanding of traditional and Digital PR and how they can be used to create waves."

Susan Hallam MBE.

"This is a fantastic and vital aid to any entrepreneur or small business owner. I wish I could have read this when I started out! A brilliant how-to guide to achieving great results to maximise your success from PR."

Rosemary Conley, CBE.

"A classic self-helper, demystifying media for entrepreneurs so they can keep on top of fast-changing times."

Maisha Frost, business and consumer correspondent, Sunday and Daily Express.

"I highly recommend this book. Without question, it's the perfect read for small business leaders who need a simple and inspiring guide into how PR can work for them. The up-to-date digital advice and case studies are very helpful.

I'll be changing my approach to PR and am excited to start work with my team to integrate more of this discipline into our business. Thanks, Louise!"

Matt Jones, Sipcam Home and Garden Ltd.

"I will be recommending this book to the start-ups I work with. They need to take Louise's advice and think about how they can apply PR to their sales and marketing activities.

I have known Louise for many years and am pleased to see her sharing her considerable experience in an accessible form for small businesses and start-ups. I particularly like how she refers to actual examples of entrepreneurs who use PR every day".

James Murdoch, Angel Investor, Director, Business Adviser, Journalist, and Author of 'Diary of a Serial Equity Crowdfunder'

Contents

Fans of PR on a Beermat 1
Contents 3
Hello from Louise Third MBE 4
Hallam 5
All about Beermat 6
Preface to this edition (2021) 7
1. What is PR and What is it For? 9
2. Thinking about PR for your Business 20
3. Types of PR 24
4. Have You Got News For Us? 27
5. Five Classic Ways to Make News 39
6. Working with News Media 51
7. Getting your Press Release right 56
8. Yikes! I'm being Interviewed! 63
9. Creating your Own Content 67
10. Networking 79
11. Digital PR – Maximise and Measure 82
12. Skills for DIY PR 89
13. Your PR Campaign 95
14. Crisis Management 102
15. Internal PR 108
16. Choosing a PR Consultancy 111
17. PR in Action 117
18. And finally… 121
Special thanks to… 124
Contacts 125

3

Hello from Louise Third MBE

Promoting the virtues of starting and growing a business has dominated my career for the past 38 years. From leafleting redundant miners in North Tyneside in the mid-1980s to running national PR campaigns encouraging more women into business, I believe in enterprise and the opportunities it can unleash.

In my teens, I was inspired by the writings of the statistician and economist E F Schumacher, especially his 1973 publication *Small is Beautiful – A study of Economics as if People Mattered*. I became fascinated by the concept of Intermediate Technology based on smaller working units, regional or community ownership, and the use of local labour and resources.

Between 2001 and 2018, I ran Integra Communications, the PR company specialising in all things entrepreneurial. Every day, I worked with the media to educate, inspire, and encourage the public about enterprise and the joys of being your own boss.

Now I am flying solo as a communications consultant doing what I enjoy most, and with the clients I love.

Want to know more? Look me up at louisethird.com or connect with me on LinkedIn.

Hallam

Hallam is a digital agency with offices in Nottingham, London, Leeds, and Malaga (Spain). Since 2000, the company has grown by providing clients with integrated and strategic digital marketing services.

The company won ten awards at The Drum Recommends Digital Awards 2020 and is the first agency to win three back-to-back Grand Prix awards, making Hallam the UK's most recommended digital marketing firm for three successive years.

Two of Hallam's digital PR experts have contributed to this book. They are Tom Bestwick and Rebecca Peel.

Tom joined the Hallam team in March 2020, arriving with seven years of PR experience, which includes four years at Derby County Football Club. He has also worked in the leisure management and retail sectors.

Rebecca has five years' experience, previously working at a technology PR agency, travelling the world raising awareness of global brands. She has recently moved to a different agency, but both she and Tom are a credit to the communications profession.

Hallam graphic designers provided the creative ideas for our cover, and I appreciate the social media support they have all offered as we take the publication from draft to your bookshelf.

All about Beermat

The book *The Beermat Entrepreneur* appeared in 2002, and I became a fan at once. It captured the spirit of small, entrepreneurial business better than any other book at the time.

The point of the beermat is that great ideas often get written on the back of a beermat in the pub, which means that they are both simple (you can't get endless lines of management-speak on a tiny cardboard rectangle) and a team business (it's assumed that the entrepreneur is not sitting alone in the pub but is there with friends). I liked that image.

The authors, Mike Southon and Chris West, went on to write a series of Beermat Guides. I got to know them, and we worked together on a Beermat Guide to PR, which was published as an eBook in 2007.

Recently, I decided it was time to revisit and revitalise this guide. To talk to a new group of business owners, consult with a fresh set of journalists, and invite some technical experts to, metaphorically, scribble on the back of a beermat.

Here it is.

Preface to this edition (2021)

Where have those 14 years gone? Back in 2007, we were oblivious to the gathering tidal wave of economic devastation that would be unleashed by the financial crash of 2008/09. We were about to enter years of public spending austerity which brought severe cuts to government-funded support for smaller firms. We were only beginning to experience the explosion of online communication platforms like Twitter, LinkedIn, Instagram, and alternative news sites – sites that would go on to threaten the very existence of the newsprint industry.

And as I write, the COVID-19 pandemic continues to wreak havoc across the economy, especially in the most vulnerable sectors like retail, hospitality, tourism, and transport. I doubt we will return to the pre-COVID way of living and conducting business, but I am an optimist. The crisis has provided new opportunities and we have seen many examples of how agile smaller businesses can quickly adapt to meet new needs. We humans adapt to survive. This is especially true of innovative and creative start-ups. That's you, or, if you are an adviser, mentor, or business friend to a start-up, the people in your care.

One thing is for sure, however. Fourteen years on, the basic principles of business – and PR – remain unchanged. Both require a clear understanding of why you are in business, who you need as customers, and a plan to get them interested in you.

That said, the tools and techniques in communication have changed beyond recognition since 2007, so to make sure you get the best up-to-date insights into digital PR, I have enlisted the help of Tom Bestwick and Rebecca Peel from award-winning digital marketing agency, Hallam. I must admit that age and a little wisdom have taught me when I need to delegate.

Our aim is that this revised Beermat guide will educate, inspire, and encourage you to get started on the PR road to successfully promoting what you do. Along the way, you will learn from five fellow entrepreneurs as well as from a few seasoned journalists, to reach the point where you are ready to leave your own PR footprint.

I have included 12 #Beermat PR Lessons. These are easy to recall and put into practice.

If you want to get noticed, you must make some noise.

Here's how.

1. What is PR and What is it For?

Why would you unleash 20 eight-foot-tall dinosaurs in the Colliers Wood branch of Sainsbury's?

Because you are Andrew Walker, founder of TEA REX fruit infusion teas. He knows a thing or two about promoting brands, and that trying to contact 69 branches of the supermarket chain would take time and most probably see his exciting new products consigned to the so-called 'development aisle', out of sight and not making any sales.

Andrew takes up the story of his daring promotional stunt which, technically illegal, went on to be embraced nationally across the store.

"Although six months in the planning, it took just 15 minutes for 20 art students dressed in dinosaur suits to cross the customer car park, enter the busy store, pose by our TEA REX display in the beverage aisle, and exit quickly before we risked being escorted from the premises. Of course, we had strategically positioned 12 friends around the displays, including a film producer, to capture the action in high-quality film ready for release. Within 48 hours the clip reached 150,000 hits on our social media channels, and I got a call from Sainsbury's early the next morning. The Colliers Wood store manager had shared it on the company's internal *Yammer* group, so we were seen by all 69 managers."

Andrew has ambitious plans for the company he started in 2016 as a challenger to the fruit tea market, which he considered bland and boring. He has built PR into the very DNA of the brand so that what he likes to call 'conversational marketing' raises a smile with his audiences. We will pick up his story as we start to develop the case for PR as a tool that every business owner can use.

What is PR, anyway?

Let's face it, some of us can be a little cynical about PR. It is a communications tool that can be abused as much as it is valued. It's often linked to people who exaggerate stories, spend half their working lives taking people out to lunch, and harassing journalists. It can be too closely associated with spin, the manipulation of facts, the wilful burying of bad news, and, occasionally, fake news.

"Just a public relations exercise" is the ill-considered, throw-away comment which is too often used to dismiss a whole profession as flighty, shallow, and underhand.

This stereotype is, like most such stereotypes, miles off the truth. PR is a serious business discipline and one that can be of huge benefit to start-ups and small businesses like yours. PR can massively increase the awareness of your brand among your target audience, but it can do much more than that.

PR can build your reputation in your industry and with the public as well as make your staff glad they are one of the team. PR can also help retrieve your reputation if something goes wrong.

Of increasing importance, PR can generate online content that helps internet search engines to find you - otherwise known as search engine optimisation (SEO). We will cover this topic in more detail later.

I've seen small firms and charities of many kinds flourish when PR has been put to good use.

So, what is it, exactly?

My professional institute, the Public Relations and Communications Association (PRCA), uses this description:

Public Relations is all about the way organisations communicate with the public, promote themselves, and build a positive reputation and public image.

It adds:

The way an organisation is represented in the media has a huge impact on how people perceive it. PR professionals try to influence the media to represent their organisation positively and communicate key messages.

Another organisation that represents the PR profession is the Chartered Institute of Public Relations (CIPR). In a similar but slightly different vein, the CIPR uses this description:

PR is the application of a planned and sustained programme of communications between an organisation and those audiences essential to its success.

Like most definitions from professional bodies, these are a little wooden, but they contain important truths that merit further scrutiny.

PR is planned. PR is part of a much bigger picture: the entire sales and marketing effort of your business. These should all be planned rather than random. Sadly, too much PR is done without much thought. While an element of opportunism can be helpful, you can't beat a properly thought-through campaign for generating real, lasting results.

PR is sustained. PR works best over time. I prefer to work with clients for at least six months and ideally up to three years, depending on the project objective and budget. I have been working with my best clients for much longer than that. Yes, there are odd one-off pieces of work that have a clear start and finish point (for example the launch of a book) – but even here, a launch is much better seen as the start of a campaign to promote both the book and everything else the author does.

We are talking about building a reputation, and there are no shortcuts to that. There may be the odd lucky break that, like landing on the right square in snakes and ladders, hastens the process. But people are easily distracted – what is in their minds one day will be replaced with something different the next. You need to keep on top of the media cycle and stay on people's radars.

Note that the word *communications* in the definition is in the plural. This isn't just about 'getting into magazines', though that is clearly one outcome of PR. We will be exploring the many ways you can 'make some noise'.

The word *audiences* is also in the plural. You might assume your main audience is your customers, current and potential. But there are other groups of people almost as important to the success of your business. How about the suppliers you rely on, your finance provider(s), the local council, and as your business grows, your employees? PR people call them 'publics' and another commonly used term, especially by politicians, is stakeholders. The relative importance of these various audiences will vary from business to business. Some businesses are very dependent on strong reputations and local goodwill, others less so. None can afford to ignore these other audiences entirely.

All in all, PR is about *getting your business noticed*, in the way you want it to be noticed. Many small businesses do it badly or not at all, so by taking a little time to read this book and acting on what it suggests, you should give yourself a healthy competitive advantage.

Andrew Walker of TEA REX defines PR as 'conversational marketing'.

I like that!

What kinds of things might you use PR for?
- Announcing a new product or service
- Announcing your company growth
- Growing your profile in your industry
- Growing your profile in your target market
- Launching an event or campaign
- Getting your brand in front of the right journalists
- Increasing your rankings on Google.

Social Media

Social media, naturally, plays a key part in modern PR. However, it is still often the case in larger organisations that the social media and PR departments very rarely talk. This is odd. They should. A lot. So, here's your opportunity to steal a march on the 'big fish' media and get this right from the start. We will look at how social and PR intertwine, but first, ask yourself one question: are you using your business' social media channels to full effect?

Is PR for me?

Considering the above, my answer is obviously, 'yes. Definitely.'

However, PR is more necessary for some businesses than for others. It can also be easier to do for some businesses than for others.

Those companies that sell services, in decent-sized chunks, to other businesses are not in desperate need of PR. Their sales cornerstone (read *The Beermat Entrepreneur* to understand cornerstones) should be making friends among as many key potential customers as possible. The rest of the team should be busy acting as ambassadors for the business, networking (more of that later), telling the world how great the company is, and looking for sales leads.

Formal PR campaigns are not at the forefront of such a business' priorities – though you could argue that every piece of networking where a team member speaks positively about the company is a tiny bit of very good PR. But please note that, even in these sectors, the smartest entrepreneurs think at least partially in PR terms. The first 'Beermat' company, The Instruction Set, was a classic B2B services business but took at least one tool out of the PR toolbox and used it repeatedly to great effect – the 'expert author' technique.

On the other hand, a business that sells small things or services to consumers like you and me must raise public awareness quickly, and PR is *the* tool for doing this.

This is especially true if you sell direct – for example, specialist shops, restaurants, tourist attractions, and lifestyle businesses from acupuncturists to florists – but PR is also essential to a business that sells to the public via retail outlets.

Businesses dealing in highly technical solutions can use PR effectively too, using the media to talk to others in their industry as well as to the public. They work hard to use plain language whilst staying true to the science or technology.

A few years ago, I reported on a major international gathering of dentists and academics in Nottingham. The presentations on digital dentistry and facial aesthetics were complex. So, for general interest, I focused on the impact the science would make on a visit to the dentist.

Radical improvements to the way dental care is delivered will be on show this week as the city plays host to some of the world's leading figures in dentistry and dental technology. The impact of their work will soon be felt the world over – from the rapid production of crowns to digital facial re-modelling and computer-aided designed bridge restoration.

I included a quote from one of the experts:

"Thursday's event is all about patient care and well-being. Better quality dental devices mean we can design treatment for individual patients that is delivered more quickly and efficiently. For people facing major dental and facial work, this will bring profound benefits in the future."

Businesses involved in health and the environment can get particularly good leverage from PR. Everyone concerned about potentially life-threatening issues will sit up and listen if a solution might benefit them. We saw this during 2020 as medical research labs around the world raced to find an effective vaccine for COVID-19.

Charity PR campaigns are crucial if these organisations are to keep up their good work. I volunteer for the Teso Development Trust (TDT), a relief and development charity working in a remote region of northeast Uganda. On our visits, we make sure we gather stories of lives changed by access to fresh water, medicines, and affordable education. These stories help donors to relate to those they are helping.

I'm impressed by the many creative ways in which professional companies like accountants, solicitors and insurance brokers use PR. After all, they are offering very similar services, governed by nationally recognised codes of practice, and they are selling sophisticated products to non-specialist buyers. Such businesses often use paid-for PR via advertorials (more on this below) or take to sponsoring events or awards (more on this later too).

Some entrepreneurs are PR naturals: born self-publicists. They are quick to spot a news angle about themselves and their venture and are fearless in approaching the media or broadcasting for themselves. This energy is best when channelled into a proper, structured PR campaign. People can have too much of a good thing and soon tire of endless, slightly random postings on LinkedIn and Twitter by the same individuals.

However, I strongly believe that with the right approach – a mixture of rigour and imagination – **any** business can come up with good quality PR and will benefit from it.

Beermat PR Lesson #1

PR is for me and my new venture

While PR is a great tool for building brand awareness and achieving high-quality coverage and links, combining it with an effective social media strategy, especially if you are a new company, will allow you to improve engagement with your audience *on a personal level* and gather valuable data and insights.

Meet the Entrepreneurs

PR is driven by stories. So, as well as TEA REX, I'd like you to meet four more entrepreneurs and their businesses. I shall be checking out their views on, and experiences of, PR at points in this book. Each represents a different sector and customer base, so whatever venture you are planning, you should find PR ideas to apply.

Tuneless Choir
In 2016, when Nadine Cooper launched the first Tuneless Choir, the media was fascinated by such a different take on singing together.

Nadine says: 'We run choirs for Tuneless people. Those lacking the ability, practice, or confidence to sing in tune. Many have been told by teachers, vicars, or their own families that they can't sing. But they love doing so anyway.

Our customers love singing and want some of the benefits that group singing can bring to their lives. The physical benefits, the mental health benefits, the social benefits. They may want to exercise their lungs, overcome anxiety, de-stress, meet new friends, or just put a bit more fun back in their lives.

Many, but not all, are women. Although we range in age from late teens to 90-odd, many Tuneless Choir members are in their 40s, 50s, and 60s."

Nadine's idea caught the imagination of both singers and the media. By early 2020 the company had grown to 30 franchises across the UK.

The Bottle Top
In 2019, husband and wife team Anthony and Alex Preston left their full-time jobs in hospitality to open The Bottle Top, a high street and online craft beer and zero-waste shop. Turnover in the first year was just over £100 thousand. The offering now includes a licensed café provided by another local business owner.

During the pandemic lockdown, The Bottle Top was considered an essential business and remained open, taking online orders and meeting shoppers at the door. These new ways of shopping and socialising meant that Anthony and Alex decided to change the way the business operated: to provide a community hub of which people felt a part. Morning customers are now served barista coffees and bakes. The afternoon and evening trade caters to lovers of locally crafted beer, ciders, and gins, who are seated outdoors. Staples such as plastic-free fruit and veg, bread and sundries are on sale all day.

Alex says: "Customers are mostly local people from the immediate village and neighbouring area. They tend to be, for the most part, 30–50 years old with a generous disposable income. They like to support independent, small businesses, are concerned for the environment, and want to buy local produce. We also operate online where we find our customers are largely craft beer enthusiasts. We have plans to grow our online sales which currently account for around five per cent of turnover."

Alpkit

Launched in 2004, Alpkit is a direct-to-consumer outdoor and bike brand. The company designs and manufactures performance clothing and equipment in the UK for runners, hikers, climbers, campers, swimmers, and bikers. There are currently eight Alpkit stores each of which organises local talks, rides, and runs. The annual Alpkit Big Shakeout is a weekend of adventure and entertainment for 1,000 outdoor enthusiasts.

The company currently generates annual sales of £8 million and has created 85 jobs. One per cent of all sales go to the Alpkit Foundation, an independent charity set up to remove barriers to getting outdoors and experiencing wild places.

Alpkit has honed its marketing and PR to a simple message: celebrate and conserve the outdoors with excellent, sustainable products, and give back.

CEO and Co-Founder David Hanney says: "From day one, Alpkit has tried to do things the right way. We're advocates of the highest ethical standards and have always chosen the most environmentally preferable methods of production. We make affordable mountain gear without compromise to performance or sustainability. Our customers are outdoor enthusiasts and, like them, we share a love of the outdoors and a belief in nature."

Lindhurst Engineering

'Engineering innovation' best describes the work of this Midlands company. Trading since 1985, the firm employs 38 people and has a current turnover of £3.75 million. There are four aspects to Lindhurst's work, which cover the fabrication of mechanical components: bespoke manufacturing of complete machines; onsite installation of machinery; maintenance and repair; and research and development (R&D) services.

Managing Director Martin Rigley MBE has led the team at Lindhurst for 26 years. He says: 'We use PR to raise our standing within our sector by spreading the message about the great work we feel we do. We use PR to promote our Corporate Social Responsibility (CSR) activities." He adds: "I feel far more comfortable shouting about helping someone else than I do about promoting the excellent engineering work we do."

2. Thinking about PR for your Business

PR is part of your overall sales and marketing strategy. So, make sure you have that strategy in place first.

The strategy doesn't have to be complex, even though some business books might make it appear so. It begins with understanding who you are, who your customers are, what you do for them, and what makes you special.

A neat tool for achieving this understanding is the Beermat Elevator Pitch. This has three elements.

Pain. What 'pain' do you solve, and for whom?
Premise. How do you do it?
Proof. Why should people buy from you rather than other people?

The answers to the questions in these three elements must underpin your PR campaigns: what you want to say, to whom, and how.

I also think it helps to use another 'triad': your **Mission, Vision, and Values.** Make these clearly understood and you will get the tone as well as messaging of your reputation-building work spot on.

To quote author and speaker Simon Sinek: "People don't buy *what* you do: they buy *why* you do it."

I offer my own business, Integra Communications, as an example. Back in 2001, we asked ourselves the pain, premise, and proof questions for our new venture. We pulled the answers into our Mission, Vision and Values.

Our Mission: To contribute to a thriving economy.
Note the use of the term *'contribute'*, which tells you that Integra intends to work in partnership with others. *'A thriving economy'* is one in which equality of opportunity, environmental impact, and the fair distribution of wealth is crucial.

Our Vision: To see our clients flourish.
We used to 'see' deliberately because it implies we expect evidence. *'Clients'* includes the ones we invoice and the charities we help on a pro bono basis. *'Flourish'* is just a great picture of all-round well-being.

Our Values: We apply wisdom and integrity to the use of PR.
'Wisdom' because 25 years in business has made us a teeny bit wiser, and *'integrity'* because it's the only way to win the trust and respect of clients and partners alike.

My business partner and I took time to think about the ethos of our business before we launched the company. I strongly suggest you do the same. Have fun imagining the part your new venture plays in sorting customers' problems, whether you offer a service or a product.

Make your answers unique. As a human being, you are unique, anyway. Harness that. When it comes to getting the attention of the media, your background, what you are doing, why you do it, and for whom, by the very laws of nature, must be different from anyone else.

Beermat PR lesson #2
My new venture and I are both unique

So, let's make some noise!

Well no. Not yet. We need to get some building blocks in place first.

The audience
Assuming you've created your overall marketing strategy, you will know who your target customers are: vets, teenagers, lawyers, retail buyers, people moving house, people who say they can't sing – or whatever: the potential is only limited by your imagination. You will have decided the finer details such as their age, where they live, and how they behave.

Target them. However, don't forget others whose respect and following you need to rely on too: existing clients, suppliers, potential employees, and influencers, such as the local MP and elected councillors. You will need a different communications approach for each group.

The message
In your marketing plan, you will have worked hard on those key messages: the mission, vision, and values of the company we discussed earlier. Stick to those three key points and *keep repeating them*. Repetition is important. In one campaign over seven years, we repeatedly described our client (factually correctly) as 'the UK's fastest-growing bioscience business incubator'. When a leading financial daily newspaper started using these exact words in their reporting, we knew the penny had dropped.

The media
Then you need the means of getting your message to your target audience. These are your target media. Make sure that you do your research. Nobody likes getting irrelevant emails in their inbox. If you send the news to a journalist who hasn't been targeted properly, it can annoy them, potentially ruining your chances of getting coverage. I recently spotted a Tweet by an irritated Lancashire reporter in response to a pitch about a Yorkshire business: "Wrong side of the Pennines, love." Ouch!

Here's a simple Venn diagram to illustrate how the audience, message, and media – the three basic principles of a PR campaign – relate to each other. Where the three circles overlap in the middle, you have your ideal PR campaign. Bullseye! This way you can target your limited resources to avoid wasting time and effort.

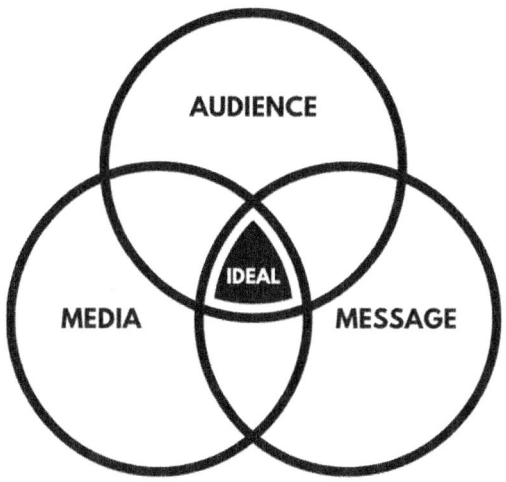

Of course, even the best-laid plans can be thrown off course by situations beyond your control, but at least you are starting with a simple plan. Sadly, many start-up businesses don't even bother with first principles and take a more shotgun, cavalier approach to PR.

Beermat PR lesson #3
Target, target, target.

23

3. Types of PR

We've looked at the triad of the audience, message, and media. Here is another essential threesome – the main types of PR. These are:

- earned publicity
- paid-for publicity
- owned and shared publicity.

Earned publicity
This is the pot of gold at the end of the publicity rainbow. It is what you, and millions of PR account managers or executives, work hard to achieve. Not only have you managed to get your information to the right person and make them sit up and read, but they have decided to run it. It is, to use an essential term, 'news': something interesting and in some way novel that the editor considers will add value for their readers. I shall use 'readers' to cover all kinds of audience: readers of a magazine, on - or off-line, listeners to a podcast, viewers of a vlog, and so on.

You have earned the right to free, impartial, thoroughly checked-out coverage. Readers will, at some level, understand that your information has passed this crucial test.

The added advantage of today's digital news-generating machine is that your coverage will stick around for a long time and won't become tomorrow's chip paper, as it did back in the Dark Ages of PR when I started my career.

Paid-for publicity
This term covers spend on advertising, PPC (pay per click), sponsorship, and advertorials. It is any activity where you have handed over well-earned cash for the privilege of a mention.

Sadly, much print PR now falls into this category. Thumb through any free paper or trade magazine and you'll see an awful lot of the content has been paid for. There should be a small print banner stating that this is a PROMOTION, and there will be full contact details for the company at the end. Nowadays, it's a major way print and online media organisations survive, as the income from direct advertising and subscription revenues dwindle.

An example. You send a press release about your move to new premises to a magazine. You get a call back from them. The conversation starts amicably with, "Thank you for sending us your press release about your move. We'd like to run the story."

You get excited. But then the voice on the other end introduces himself as Terry from the ad sales team.

Basically, your release has not proven amazing enough for the magazine to want to run it for free. They want to charge you. Terry continues without taking a breath, "We do need to add a small charge for colour separation."

Years ago, someone in the print warehouse would have to work hard to reproduce your image or photo to get it ready for print. So, there was a cost to the colour separation task. Today's digital print technology has done away with such time-consuming and costly work: no payment is necessary. What Terry really means is that your story hasn't passed muster with the editorial team and is, instead, a possible money-earner for the commercial sales team.

Now you have a choice. Either you politely tell Terry you don't have an ad budget, or you negotiate. Yes, you can negotiate, especially if you know that the publication is close to closing the edition, has page space to fill, and is where you want to be seen. Never pay the full advertising rate. Negotiating is all part of the process of getting coverage.

I'm sure you realise that this kind of publicity is less impressive than earned publicity, but it still gets your message across in a medium that is respected by its readers.

Owned and shared publicity

There is a further way to get noticed – a route many businesses now take, especially on social media. You self-publish.

This way, you are the editor. You control the coverage. Whether it's a news item, an article, a blog, a video (vlog), or a thought-leader comment, it can be on the internet at the press of a button. The downside? Readers know that you are talking about your own business. The upside? If you develop a conversation with your audience, build bonds, and show an interest in them, they'll like and share your posts. You get noticed, and this can lead to building the reputation and potential sales you seek.

So, each type of PR has its good and bad sides. I shall be looking at all three types throughout this book.

4. Have You Got News For Us?

I mentioned news in the context of earned publicity, adding that this is the best kind of coverage. So how do you get it?

With apologies to the popular BBC TV programme, I've developed a workshop for entrepreneurs, which I co-present with a journalist. We call it *'Have You Got News for Us?'* During the session, delegates learn all about what does and doesn't make news. They spend time in small groups drafting a press release to pitch to my co-presenter, who acts as an editor. In a constructive, and at times frank, exchange, the journalist skilfully unpicks the stories and effectively teaches the novice business-owner PRs to appreciate what editors and journalists are looking for in a story. My trainees leave with a better appreciation of the work of the editor. They are also better prepared to improve, defend, or even concede defeat and ditch their news pitch.

News must be about 'things happening', such as the opening of a shop or the launch of a book. It doesn't have to be big things – the appointment of someone new is news: it's not headline-grabbing stuff, so don't pretend it is. News is an unusual event, like a customer with an unusual problem that you solved imaginatively. Always have at the back of your mind the key messages you honed as you started to plan your communications. How will the news enhance that reputation if it's covered?

I mentioned editors and journalists. The job of the *journalist* is to report events as they happen. They are also searching for new ways to explain and illustrate trends, for example, the decline of the high street or the switch to electric vehicles. The *editor* is then tasked with selecting the most important news for their readers and honing pieces so they are told as well as they can be.

For the national press, journalists are the way in. For the trade press or specialist sites, it is usually the editor who you speak to – though this is not a rule.

In either case, these people get hundreds of emails a day, so before you contact them, it's important to identify what they find newsworthy. I asked a business correspondent at the *Daily Mail*, Tom Witherow, for his views.

He said that business stories are broadly categorised into two groups – 'human interest' and 'hard news' stories.

Human interest could be the tale about how a business owner came back from hardship to start the business and make a success of it. Or it could be an amazing thing they've done in the community. For these stories, the key ingredients are (a) biographical – readers want to know details about the person's life, with (b) the challenge they faced, giving details about key moments the reader can relate to. And (c) strong pictures to illustrate the point.

Hard news, on the other hand, consists of events like the release of financial results or statistics from a survey or company recruitment data, together with a commentary from an expert on the topic and the opportunity for the journalist to add an analysis of the facts as part of the coverage.

A business in its early years will most likely pitch stories to local newspapers, television, and radio. Journalists will be looking for stories rooted in their local community, so you need to look for ways that their audience will identify with your business from a geographical point of view. That might be living there for a long time, starting a business rooted in the area's history, or providing much-needed jobs for locals.

Think about what makes your business unique or unusual? Is it run by three sisters? Do you operate from a historic building? Are you offering employment to ex-offenders as retailer Timpson does, or to people who used to be homeless or refugees? Are you a small business that has just gained a large national client?

Things that are less interesting (and Tom gets a lot of these) include more corporate affairs like mergers and acquisitions, attracting venture capital, and share price rises. Readers want human stories first and foremost, but of course, some publications thrive on technical business news.

Take a look at the questions below. They will help you to weed out topics that are not very interesting and will help you to identify things going on in your business that are worth shouting about.

- Have you won any interesting contracts? Can you talk about them?
- What do you think of the recent news in your industry? Can you comment on it?
- What is the current situation with your customers? Are you noticing any changes in behaviour?
- Have you recently made any big hires?
- Have you recently won any awards or worked on a project with someone of high influence?
- Are there any new regulations you can comment on?
- Do you have any business or customer data you can share?

During the COVID-19 crisis, many smaller firms were forced to pivot their offering and cater for newly emerging consumer needs. Social media was full of their stories and brought some light relief to lockdown news-surfing. Here is the story of how an enterprising couple in Nottinghamshire responded to this challenge, achieving media coverage and admiration for their community spirit. Pun intended.

A Ruddy Fine response to beat the Covid-19 virus

Gin-lovers Cheryl Stretton and Rory Thorpe were both running successful, well-established businesses in the Nottinghamshire village of Ruddington when the Covid-19 crisis led to a nationwide lockdown in March 2020. For several years they had been tinkering around with steeping and making their own gins in a little copper still in their kitchen in Ruddington as a hobby, but due to the pressure of work, this was as far as they had gone.

When the first lockdown came, they took the opportunity to bring their dreams to life. They wasted no time in purchasing and installing their still, 'Marion', and began obtaining the licenses. Whilst waiting for the documentation, and hearing of the worldwide shortage in hand sanitiser, they saw a great opportunity to 'do their bit'. They fired up Marion.

Following the World Health Organisation (WHO) recommended formula for hand sanitising gel to 'kill' COVID-19, they started producing Ruddy Fine Hand Sanitiser using their equipment and new-found know-how.

Cheryl admits that any thoughts of making money out of the new venture were put on hold: "We wanted to help the vulnerable in our area, as there was such a shortage of hand sanitiser. We wanted people to be protected as much as possible against this deadly disease and we were able to help. So, the first two hundred bottles were donated to the local community and the rest sold at cost, just covering the materials, not our time or overheads."

As well as achieving some great media coverage, their MP gave them a mention in the House of Commons.

They eventually started making their craft gins. A variety of flavours began rolling off the distillery production line in July 2020. First London Dry and Summer Berries Pink Gin, followed by an old-school Navy Strength and their Christmas Gin, which sold out in less than 30 days.

> With the launch of their website and The Ruddy Fine Gin Club, Cheryl and Rory hope to capitalise on the very positive and loyal following they have generated through their willingness to help during the Covid crisis.
>
> ruddyfine.co.uk

News can also be you

Many entrepreneurs' eyes light up when I say this – but please approach this opportunity with caution. News is not your ego, or about how wonderful you are. It can be your story, and it can be your views but only if they are original, relevant and you express them well.

Your story

One of the first exercises I set on the *'Have You Got News for Us'* workshop is to ask everyone to write down the story of themselves and their business. Often the stories are excellent. Journalists will be particularly interested in things like:

- Your background, especially your upbringing and relevant interests.
- What gave you the idea in the first place?
- Where has the business got to now (size, employees, turnover, etc.)?
- Any special people who have helped you.
- Was anyone particularly negative?
- What was your biggest lucky break?
- Were there any 'epiphanies? For example, my first business venture was selling homemade lemonade to thirsty walkers in a quiet Derbyshire lane. I was about six at the time. Then I realised I could make double the money by selling water (which is free) to owners of horses passing by my house.

- Were there any moments when things looked like they were heading down the pan – and what did you do to turn things around?
- What have you learned?
- Where's the business going now?

If you struggle to write your story fluently, don't give up. Use bullet points or keep an audio diary to remind you of the key points. The rest can be expressed in a media interview if you manage to bag one.

Having your story ready for use by a journalist is very helpful and saves you time later too. Editors will be looking for topical and timely content to add colour to a current news story, which will help the reader or listener to relate to the item being reported. Your profile and willingness to comment might be exactly what they need. Next time you pick up your local paper or trade magazine, look at how often a writer has used stories and comments from people like you and me to drive home the main point of the feature.

Your views

Mainstream media, as well as trade press, are always looking out for people within a given profession who can come up with original comments on important issues in a clear, distinct, and entertaining way. The newspaper has become the 'views paper'. The Institute of Directors' *Director* magazine ran a popular column for years, written by Chris West, explaining the Beermat view of things. That's how I got to know him and his co-author, Mike Southon. The rest is Beermat history.

It takes time to get to know editors and to get them to regard you as a reliable source of information and a quality expert – but it's time well spent. More on this relationship-building process later.

News that you make

Finally, and very importantly, news can be made. What can you do in your PR activity to raise a smile and encourage that feel-good reaction to your business?

The story I recounted at the beginning of this book shows how TEA REX achieved massive PR from their own creative efforts by staging the dinosaur drop-in at Sainsbury's. What could you do?

- Classic news-creation activities like sponsorship, writing a book, attending exhibitions, and winning awards. I shall go into these in greater detail in the next chapter.

- Surveys. Carry out a survey of customers and see if any information comes out that is of general interest. Talk to some journalists and their eyes might roll at the idea of another survey, but the reality is that your findings could shed light on a problem or issue that needs discussing. Journalists do need facts and statistics – of course, they will check for accuracy. Ideally, at least 500 people should be surveyed to make it authoritative.

- Events. Organise an event – a special night at your restaurant, an exhibition at your workshop, a lecture on aromatherapy, etc.

- Stunts. These must be handled with care and only suit certain businesses. A stunt can be a risky undertaking and requires careful research, planning, and execution. Ask yourself what could possibly go wrong? Stunts can work very well for charity campaigns and consumer business offerings. So, if that's your business, and there are a lot of excellent businesses in that category, then why not have a try? Remember how we started with the TEA REX stunt at Sainsbury's? It was carefully planned to have a commercial impact, so Andrew Walker's advice is that it needs to be: "A prank, or a stunt, with a purpose".

- Case Studies are very popular with the trade press: how I solved problem X for customer Y. Back to my suggestion that you keep a diary from the moment you have the idea to the launch of the business and beyond. It's amazing what you will forget in the busy business of running a business.

- Campaigns are a powerful PR tool if you and your company feel strongly about something. Campaigns try to change decisions, attitudes, and behaviours.

The #MicroBizMatters campaign was started by author and business leader Tony Robinson OBE and business partner Tina Boden. It has succeeded in getting greater recognition for the UK's 5.6 million micro-businesses (ones that employ up to nine people).

Launched in January 2015 with a very limited PR budget, Tony and Tina got the support of celebrity entrepreneurs who joined in lobbying for a better understanding of the issues faced by these firms. Tony said: "We hope that eventually there will be an announcement that the Prompt Payment Code which large companies (over 250 employees) sign up to, will move from pay in 60 days to #PayIn30Days. This would release £25 billion to micro business owners twice as fast."

#MicroBizMatters has subsequently become a movement to champion, support, speak for, and celebrate those whose efforts contribute so much to the UK economy.

- Competitions are especially effective if your business serves a local market. Let's say you run the local golf club and your members decide to hold an annual competition to raise funds for charity.

Make money, and headlines, for a serious cause by organising a fun day that everyone, including non-golfers, can get involved in.

- Links to special months, weeks, and days can make something into news. This will ensure that your news is topical and timely, both of which are crucial if you are heading the news desk and need that 'And finally…' item.

Make time to consult 'Year Ahead', published by Profile Group, or simply search online, and use your judgement as to which cause-related months, weeks, days, etc. merit your serious attention. Most of them are rather absurd and will probably be treated as such by editors and journalists who know that their readers will share their scepticism: National Tiddlywinks Fortnight, Annual Cauliflower Day, and so on.

However, not all fall into this category. If the underlying issue is important, such as Breast Cancer Awareness Month (October), then the designated day or month is a useful way of reminding the busy public about it. And as such, the designation can be used to generate publicity. Here are some more examples of making news.

#ppe4nhs
In April 2020, Martin Rigley, managing director of Lindhurst Engineering, launched a regional campaign asking others to donate spare stocks of Personal Protective Equipment (PPE) in the fight against Covid infection.

As reported in *The Star* (Sheffield), Martin said: "Having worked in engineering and manufacturing for nearly 40 years, I know there will now be cupboards and storerooms full of PPE in factories, construction companies, pubs, restaurants, nail bars, hairdressers, garages, and schools. It's amazing just the diversity of businesses that use PPE in their day-to-day work. Our NHS desperately needs this PPE and, as a business community we have a duty to get it to them without putting people at risk."

Using local press, radio, and TV coverage across South Yorkshire and the East Midlands, the campaign galvanised companies into a response and organised collection points across four counties. More than 120,000 items of PPE were repurposed for use by the NHS. Martin feels that using targeted PR was key to the campaign's success, and Lindhurst's efforts were recognised by the Government and trade bodies including the Confederation of British Industry.

Hug in a Mug gift set
In 2019 Andrew Walker secured the domain name for Hug in a Mug. He liked it but wasn't sure when he'd get to use it. Then in March 2020 we all went into lockdown and couldn't see friends and family for several months. Hug in a Mug was dusted down and became a gift idea. Andrew already knew the founder of Wholey Moly giant cookies, Meenesh Mistry, and between them, they created a gift pack consisting of a TEA REX tea sachet and a Wholey Moly biscuit. £1 of every sale goes to the food poverty charity The Trussell Trust. The greetings message to the recipient appears on the outer package which means the words of encouragement and happy thoughts can be read by everyone, including the postman.

Andrew adds: "The greeting is the first thing people share on social media when they get the gift – it's been a great way to build our reputation and our following as a caring and sharing brand. It's the thought that counts: it's quicker than organising and sending a card and feels like a gift. I reckon one in five recipients has gone on to send several 'Hugs' and a number of these have been companies wanting to reach out to their remote-working staff during the pandemic."

What can you do in your PR activity to raise a smile and encourage that feel-good reaction to your business?

You may (or may not) remember a badger falling through the roof of a Superdrug store in the Grosvenor Shopping Centre in Northampton. It happened in February 2020, after the creature had climbed into the ceiling ducts to shelter from a storm. The news made national headlines, featuring in over 100 local, regional, and national publications.

The shopping centre could have left it there and basked in the glory of this unusual story, but, instead, they decided to have a little bit of fun to keep the conversation alive.

You'll be pleased to know the badger survived, but a few days after the incident, Grosvenor Shopping launched a Facebook competition inviting the community to name the badger that fell through the roof. They offered a £20 Superdrug voucher to the winner as an added incentive.

Solely from a social media perspective, the post was the shopping centre's best-performing post of the year, achieving 194 likes, 327 comments, and 62 shares.

It didn't just stop at social media, however. After launching the content on Facebook, the links and details were sent to the shopping centre's local media partners, leading to an article in the Northampton Chronicle and an interview on BBC Radio Northampton.

To maintain momentum, the winning name for the badger was announced live in another separate interview on BBC Radio Northampton, which was later repeated on Greg James' Radio 1 Breakfast Show, reaching millions of people across the UK. The winning name was Baffle.

After Baffle got his name, a local business created a limited number of fridge magnets to commemorate the unusual event, while a plaque was erected outside the Superdrug store, ensuring a regular stream of news content about the event for the rest of the month.

Clearly, the shopping centre's press team, aided by Baffle, knew how to *make news*.

Can you do the same?

> **Beermat PR Lesson #4**
> News should be topical and timely

5. Five Classic Ways to Make News

Now let's explore five classic ways to make news: sponsoring something, public speaking, writing a book, exhibitions, and entering awards.

Sponsorship
Don't assume that sponsorship deals start with loads of noughts: you might find that as little as £100 for a local prize gets you on the first rung of the sponsorship ladder and merits some publicity. The key to successful sponsorship activity is to find the right fit with your core values. Back to those values we covered in Chapter Two.

Keep control of the sponsorship process by entering into a clear contract with those you are supporting. Before you arrange the bank transfer, ask yourself the following questions:

Who or what should we be associated with? Become familiar with the opportunities that exist locally in the education, charity, community, and business sectors, and choose one that you feel strongly about. Beware of backing political or controversial causes, and always check out all potential recipients of your philanthropy to make sure there are no skeletons in their cupboards.

It is better to focus on one sector, and probably just one project, to start with, rather than take a scatter-gun approach by giving smaller amounts to many projects.

What should we spend? If you run an upmarket fashion shop, a £500 prize for the top fashion school graduate at your local college ought to achieve decent editorial coverage in local and regional press, compared with spending the equivalent on a one-page advert in a regional glossy magazine.

Fix an annual sponsorship budget with clear parameters and review your spending and its impact at the end of each year.

What do we get for the sponsorship? You must agree on clear terms such as free tickets for an event, regular PR, a speaking slot, or exclusivity.

Growing businesses will notice that sponsorship can have a strongly positive effect on staff morale. Encourage colleagues to nominate the cause. Individuals might represent your company at awards events or on local committees; you could pay staff for giving their time to the charity or activity. People will feel valued and respect the company more. It can also be a good angle for a media story, too.

Here's a checklist for your sponsorship agreement:

- Specify the amount of money or help-in-kind being given.
- Specify the duration.
- Agree on how the funding will be applied.
- Agree on all the detailed extras such as guest tickets, speaking slots, use of logos, press releases, etc.
- Appoint someone to oversee your sponsorship, if not yourself.
- Sign and date the agreement.
- Review whether your objectives were met.

David Hanney and his team have applied these sponsorship principles to their *Alpkit Big Shakeout*, a weekend of adventure and entertainment held annually in the Derbyshire Peak District attracting more than 1,000 lovers of the outdoors. The non-profit event raises funds for the Alpkit Foundation, a charity set up by the company to give small grants to people, groups, and schools removing the barriers to getting outdoors and experiencing wild places.

David believes that the Big Shakeout festival is a good example of how PR works well for them. "It's an end-of-summer party, quite unique and a celebration of the great outdoors. Our customers love it, and the staff get involved from serving behind the bars, in the food stalls, or running the School of Adventures, to cleaning the toilets and emptying bins. The spirit at midnight in the main tent when the bands are playing, people are dancing and having a good time is wonderful. I know that our brand cannot fail with followers like this."

It seems David is right about the value of his followers and how PR has built Alpkit's reputation. When the company launched an investment campaign on the crowdfunding platform CrowdCube in June 2020, it hit its target of £750,000 in just eight minutes. The maximum investment cap of £1.5 million was achieved 44 minutes later, and at its peak, five people were investing every second. Many of the 1,380 new shareholders are Alpkit customers, some investing as little as £10 but eager to have a stake in the business they have come to feel part of.

On the other hand, Alex from The Bottle Top has learned that sponsorship doesn't always work out. "Our joint sponsorship of a female-led book launch was not as successful as hoped. We joined two other companies in sponsoring the launch event for an anthology of female authors who had overcome adversity to run successful businesses. It was quite costly and unfortunately didn't result in much publicity or bounce back to our business. After some reflection, we believe there were several reasons. The audience was more business-to-business, not our potential customers. The event was held in Leicestershire, where we were unknown to the attendees. We hadn't set out our expectations or understood the implications of sharing the glory with two other sponsors. Despite some positives, the cost versus the result was disproportionate."

Public Speaking

Speaking in public to an appreciative audience is a great way of promoting yourself and your business. Martin Rigley of Lindhurst Engineering uses speaking opportunities to share research material as well as sharing expertise on topics such as workforce development, apprenticeships, and community engagement. He has spoken at international technology conferences, networking events and government consultations.

Most of us are nervous about speaking in public so it's a good idea to get some training and plenty of practice. Here are some of the tips I share when I'm coaching speakers.

- Remember that audiences aren't there to get at you. They are there to be entertained and informed, so entertain and inform them. What can they learn from you? How might you help them?
- Why are you on your feet anyway? What do you want to achieve by putting yourself through the ordeal? Have a clear aim and your content should flow naturally?
- Make time to plan and rehearse. When I coach speakers, I always ask them to bring a draft speech they can work from. Often, they arrive on training day apologetic for not having prepared anything. Now they are under more pressure but this time of their own making. A painful first lesson.
- Learn from the ancient Greeks. They really understood how to woo a crowd. According to the philosopher Aristotle, the perfect speech is a combination of logos (the facts), ethos (your values) and pathos (some emotion).
- Be yourself. People relate to people, not lists of facts. The best speakers are those who might be a bit nervous but who are enthusiastic about their subject. You will only recall 10 per cent of what they said but they'll leave you feeling positive and maybe persuade you to do something because of their call to action.

- Have a conversation with your audience. A famous TV presenter wisely told me that speaking to a crowd of 300 is simply talking to one person 300 times.
- Don't push your products or services. Your audience will switch off instantly.
- Don't be daunted by time. Speaking for 30 minutes may seem an eternity, but if it is on a subject that you know well, it will fly by – especially as this means, in practice, 20 minutes talking, with 10 minutes for questions.
- If someone asks you a question to which you don't know the answer, apologise. Say you'll find out for them and get their contact details. That way you keep them happy, and you've made a new connection, too.
- Have a few extra points to add if nobody asks questions (unusual, but it can happen).
- It's also worth planting a question to get the Q&A flowing. The questioner is likely to oblige if you provide them with the words.
- And if you're a little nervous before you start… so is everyone else who speaks, even top pros.

There is a multitude of books and articles, as well as training courses, on speaking in public, so look around to find what's on offer.

You may take things further and develop as an expert speaker. We have all come across those individuals whose pictures and profiles grace the pages of conference brochures or who pop up as columnists on topical websites – the industry 'guru'. Could you be one? If so, please don't call yourself a 'guru' if you want to be taken seriously!

Success in this field does not necessarily go to the pushiest: be more subtle and let others come to view you as the expert. Even if you think you have become one, don't tell everyone you are the nation's number one expert;

it gets up people's noses. Provide amazing material and let them decide for themselves. Here's how to get a few speaking invitations.

- Choose one area of your work to focus on. There is too much competition for the generalist to have a chance of making an impact.
- Write a profile, outlining your industry specialism as objectively as possible, avoiding any use of superlatives.
- Identify just one or two events or workshop opportunities and contact the organiser directly with the offer of help.
- Be prepared to speak or to facilitate a meeting for free. You may be able to charge as demand for your time increases. I have hosted awards events for free initially but subsequently requested a fee to cover time and expenses.
- Network in the most influential circles of your trade; this way people get to know and trust you.
- Develop a theme or style unique to you. It might be a suitable catchphrase or even a piece of clothing. Simon Woodroffe, founder of the Yo! Sushi brand used to pace the stage in his trademark suede boots of many colours. This suited him. It got him noticed and remembered.
- You need to remain authentic though. Avoid gimmicks.

Writing a book

Authoring a book can bring immense credibility, though getting it published can be very tough.

If you do not have experience in writing, don't just plunge into tackling a full-length book. Start by writing short articles. Ask the editors who print your pieces whether they like your style, or where it can be improved. Most will be more than happy to comment.

How long should your book be? Ladey Adey, award-winning author and publisher says, "The actual length is up to you, but generally, 25,000 words or more is needed for it to be regarded as a book. This minimum number of words makes the book large enough to print the title and author's name on the spine."

She adds, "First-time writers think they have to do it all themselves. To produce the best book possible, a team needs to be created involving an editor, proofreader, beta readers, typesetter, cover designer, illustrator, and publisher. It can take a village to produce a book.

"Writing can be very lonely so take advantage of the experience of others: it's why we have an Author Mentor Programme (www.ladeyadey.com). Every author can join the Alliance for Independent Authors (ALLi), which is a brilliant source of information."

Here are some thoughts from Chris West, co-author of *The Beermat Entrepreneur*.

"If you write a book, it should be the best possible book it can be, as that will position you as someone with an opinion worth taking seriously.

"The best way to write a really good book is to get a professional to help you. This doesn't have to mean handing it over to someone else. You can get good coaching on how to structure your book and how to improve your style. Two coaches I recommend are:

- Ginny Carter, marketingtwentyone.co.uk
- Mindy Gibbins-Klein, bookmidwife.com

"If you still find writing onerous or too time-consuming, then take on a professional ghost-writer. He or she will discuss your project with you, then conduct a series of interviews with you, which they will turn into a professionally written first draft, which you can then work with them to perfect.

"If you really 'click' with a journalist, maybe, just maybe, he or she will 'ghost' your work – for an appropriate fee, of course. Alternatively, a great place to find ghostwriters is unitedghostwriters.co.uk. This is a collective of about 15 top professionals. Go on the site; check out their profiles; contact the ones you like the sound and look of.

"Chemistry is essential. If you don't click with a ghost-writer, the project won't work. But professional ghosts have good people skills. Be reasonable with them and they will be very reasonable back! They are not control freaks wanting to wrest your project out of your hands; they are there to ensure you write a great book.

"What they are not is cheap. A good ghost-writer may cost you £20,000 or more – which is why I suggest the coaching option as a starter.

"Whatever route you take, regard the money you spend on your book as a marketing cost.

"Sadly, even having a professional ghost does not guarantee publication. 'Big name' publishers are having a difficult time now and have become ever-more risk-averse. And even if you do manage to land a deal with a publisher, don't expect to make much money from it directly. It will be a great advertisement for yourself and your expertise, not a money-spinner.

"If you don't land a named publisher, do it yourself. This will involve some more expense – a professionally designed cover is a must, and even with work from a professional ghost, a proofreader will be required to minimise typos. But it is necessary. A really strong book is a fantastic advertisement for yourself and your brand."

When you do get published, using whichever route you choose, there will be PR opportunities around the launch of the book – but you will be largely responsible for making them happen. Even big publishing houses these days have little budget to help with your publicity, other than with a press release. You will need to finance, plan, and execute your own book promotion.

When I handled the media work for a new gardening book, we held a launch event in the grounds of the author's garden, with plenty of photo and interview opportunities and signed copies for sale. The fact that the author had overcome cancer and then climbed Mont Blanc for charity at the age of 68 also generated valuable public interest. We also organised a book signing session in the local branch of Waterstones, where we found ourselves alongside Deborah, the late Duchess of Devonshire, who had written a book about Chatsworth House. She certainly drew the crowds. My author went on to give lectures, which in turn attracted visitors to her garden each summer. Not quite on the scale as Chatsworth, not still locally popular.

Exhibitions
As I write, COVID-19 has halted mass gatherings, sending the huge events and exhibitions industry into something of a tailspin. Strictly speaking, attending exhibitions is part of the wider marketing mix and does not have to be covered in a book on PR. But there is a specific PR aspect to this, which I should cover. For maximum effect and return on spend, you must take advantage of any trade press interest in the event. Look for speaker opportunities, too. All those visitors need entertainment to keep them in the venue.

Very few start-ups can afford stands at major events – but go along anyway, and network as if your life depended on it. As soon as they resume in whatever format is deemed COVID-safe, make sure the dates and venues appear in your PR schedule. If you do decide to exhibit, get all the

PR mileage you can. After all, you have paid the organisers handsomely to be there. In turn, they should have tried to get the relevant trade press and freelance reporters along. Most likely there will be a special edition of the main trade magazine produced as part of the exhibition marketing materials. You need to pitch to the organiser's press office, so they help you get featured via an article or interview. Be prepared to compete with the companies that have paid to be featured. On the day, make sure the event press office gives you the names of all the editors and journalists who are due to attend. Track them down. Get your whole exhibiting team involved, not least to cover for you if you are being interviewed.

You should also try and negotiate a speaking slot. There might be a cost involved but it means you do get a platform to showcase your expertise. Most exhibitions run seminars or workshops to keep visitors on site and to add value to their attendance. For several years I was a regular speaker at the Business Start-Up Show held twice a year in the NEC Birmingham and at London Olympia. The event programme included keynote inspirational, all-singing-all-dancing speeches from those more famous than me. I preferred to deliver 30-minute technical seminars on PR to attentive, note-taking audiences of aspiring start-uppers. The seminar topics varied from how to launch a franchise to sales, marketing, and finance, but were always well attended by exhibition visitors eager to learn something new – and to rest weary legs.

Entering and winning awards
Abandon all self-doubt and enter your company for an award. TEA REX won a Great Taste Award early on in its life, receiving excellent publicity, especially within the industry. It's quite a simple process and once you get the hang of it there will be no stopping you. The process of entering will get you noticed by the awards' sponsors and judges, and short-listed candidates get their profiles across social media and into awards catalogues. You may well get a seat at the prestigious finals.

In search of content for an article, I once conducted an informal survey in the queue for the bathroom at an awards ceremony. My mission was to find out what people had gained from entering the competition. The replies, from office junior to MD, were instructive.

- 'The company had learned more about itself.'
- 'The process of entering had required internal audits, research, fact-finding, and even a little soul searching.'
- 'Key staff had learned to express in words what the company had achieved.'
- 'It's fun.'

Bedecked and bejewelled, the staff were enjoying a night out in style – and if by chance they won, they would be able to dine out on the win, both literally and metaphorically, for months to come. Most important of all, of course, was the media coverage guaranteed by such events.

The choice of awards to enter is phenomenal. Online research of your industry, a scan of the promotional literature, and personal recommendations will help you decide which ones suit your purposes.

A wise strategy is to cut your teeth on the lesser-known industry awards, then work your way up. One of the most prestigious is the Queen's Award for Enterprise www.queensawards.org.uk. The website provides a guide to the categories and how entries are submitted. The Award emblem is recognised globally as a mark of corporate quality and success and acts as a powerful marketing tool.

However, a few words of caution about the awards route to PR.

The awards industry, like so many others, has got into making money. Depending on the organiser, they may charge an entry fee, citing administration and overheads as the reason. The biggest money-spinner is the awards dinner, for which you can pay handsomely if you book a corporate table. At the same time, the dinner will most likely be sponsored by industry heavyweights with deep pockets. They will get the first shout in the PR activity when it comes to being quoted directly in any pre-event press releases. It's part of the deal with the organisers. If you win, you get your photo taken with – you guessed it – the award sponsor.

My advice is to accept this for what it has become. Chill out. Treat it as you would any other promotional cost and make the most of the business networking – and team building – on the night. But if you win, and you value your corporate reputation, be sure to nominate and prepare a colleague to collect the trophy. That colleague will have penned a few memorable lines in advance and will have abstained from alcohol. Consequently, she or he will do a sterling job and stand head and shoulders above the rest of the winning pack.

Sadly, herein lies the awards corporate-reputation-destroying trap. Forget the after-dinner comedian: I find the winner announcements section of the evening the most entertaining, but for all the wrong reasons. Picture the scene as the winning company's scapegoat rep, who has enjoyed too much of the corporate hospitality, is shoved forward by colleagues. The victim stumbles to the stage and stares out into the black auditorium abyss. Do they know what to do next? No. Is their appearance dishevelled? Yes. Have they prepared some words? No. At this point their colleagues head for the stage, taking several repeats of the cheesy muzak to reach the steps. There follows a scrum to see how many sozzled staff can get into the official photo and make the most juvenile of poses. Has anyone seen the sponsor? Or the host of the awards? No. They have wisely left the stage to protect their image and credibility.

Enough said. I hope you win and that your reputation remains intact too.

6. Working with News Media

A key to getting regular earned PR through media coverage is to have the best possible relationship with the gatekeepers: the journalists, and editors.

As a professional working in public relations, I have always taken the view that journalists and news gatherers are my colleagues, and as such we should have respect for each other's trade. Our roles are different, but we have a symbiotic relationship. We will not survive without each other. A comment from one of my journalism undergraduate interns nailed it: she looked up from her desk and said: "I had no idea PRs did so much work for reporters." I told her never to forget this. She has gone on to a very successful career within the BBC, and we are still in touch.

National business news journalists cover different sectors. So, whether you are in farming or biotech, you need to pitch to the journalist who covers your area. Tom Witherow of the Daily Mail, who we met earlier, covers retail, hospitality, leisure, and travel: you can check out his writing online and on Twitter.

Knowing the publication you are targeting is important. Local papers and broadcasters will probably have a business reporter, or maybe a news reporter who has an interest in business issues. If you don't find out who that is – by checking their website to see who writes most of the business stories – then you may be wasting your time with your pitch.

Editorial coverage
This is what you want from the media. Back to the earned PR I mentioned in Chapter 3. Your story has been picked up and run by an editor because he or she thinks it will please or inform their audience. This applies equally to local radio and regional TV as it does to online and print news media.

Regular readers, listeners, or viewers have come to trust the editor's judgement as to what will work for them. The Daily Mail reader will raise an eyebrow at the news of Britain's middle-classes behaving in unbecoming ways, whilst The Guardian reader will want every detail in the complexities of the societal divide between North and South and their disputed boundaries.

Let's imagine you have a news item, and you think it is right for 'Practical Grommets' magazine. Boil your story down to a few sentences.

> 'It's about how we found a customer with some genuine 1873 grommets made by Jenkins Brothers, a major local employer up till about 1980. They were rusted in, so we had to take them out very carefully. We tried all sorts of ways but ended up putting my daughter's hair gel on them. That worked so we replaced them with our latest models. Then we took the old ones to the town museum and presented them to the curator, and they're going on display next month.'

Time spent getting this right so that it tells a clear story and the interesting aspects that stand out, is time well spent. Then learn your potted story, or at least have it typed out and be able to read from that in a lively and clear manner.

Tom Witherow again: "The key is to get the nub of the story across in plain English – no business jargon – in the subject line and the first line of your email to the journalist. The best tip I was ever given was to tell the first line of the story like you are shouting it across a noisy pub. If your mate Dave at the Red Lion can't 'get' the story from that first line, it needs to be written in simpler English. Use the active tense and boil it down to one or two key facts."

What do our entrepreneurs say about working with journalists?

Nadine Cooper, Tuneless Choir
"Put yourself in their shoes. They need a lot of quality content. Provide it and they'll probably be very grateful and publish. Try not to let a call from a journalist go unanswered. If they are phoning, they want to speak to you now because they have your stuff in front of them and have some questions. I'm sure I've talked to some reporters from the bathroom as I didn't want to miss the opportunity! If they ask you to be somewhere at a certain time, try your darndest to be there, rather than negotiating. And if you have to get back to them with something such as another photo, do it quickly. They need people to be easy to work with."

Alex Preston, The Bottle Top
"Building a good relationship with reporters and journalists can stand you in good stead. Our most successful PR campaigns have come from places where we have nurtured those relationships. Staying in contact regularly and submitting articles and stories that are relevant and in a good-to-go state makes the process much more successful. Having a good relationship means that you won't always need to chase them: they are more likely to chase you for a story or expert comment. We find that giving our press contacts notice of other stories, not related to us but that they may find interesting or useful, is a good way to build respect."

David Hanney, Alpkit
"Journalists and reporters are busy people working to their own pressures and deadlines. The more you can make their lives easier, the more it will help you. Give the journalist or reporter the language you want them to use. Let them know the 'why' behind what you do so that they get it straight away."

Martin Rigley, Lindhurst Engineering
"We use a marketing and PR agency because they have the media contacts and know-how to pull copy together for maximum effect. Reporters and journalists can have a habit of presenting your story to meet their needs, so a good PR agency will work to keep them on your message."

The view from the news desk

I began earlier by saying that journalists, small businesses, and their PRs should have respect for each other's roles. To know is to understand – that's my mantra. So, I asked our journalist contributors two questions: 'What three things do you like about your job?' and 'How is newsgathering likely to change by 2025?' Here is what they said:

Three things I like about my job in journalism
Natalie Fahy, editor of Nottingham Post: "I like the people, the stories, and the chase. We live and breathe our jobs. It's not a job: it's a way of life."

Maisha Frost, business, personal finance, and consumer reporter, Daily and Sunday Express: 'Having close, meaningful contact with an array of different people from all walks of life, writing stories, and through those stories making things better for them and the wider environment."

Tom Witherow, business correspondent at the Daily Mail: "Mine is a very human job – journalists build relationships quickly with people and, hopefully, earn their trust. And we must understand circumstances that we probably haven't experienced and tell those stories with sensitivity to our subjects, but also in a way that entertains and informs our audience. Sometimes it's a challenging balancing act to keep both editors and sources happy, but it's very rewarding.

"I also like the fast pace of the job and being forced to react quickly to events – it's an adrenaline rush! I feel strongly about holding powerful (and sometimes bad) people to account whether they are local councillors or chief executives of multinational corporations. It's a privilege to have some small role in giving normal people a voice when it seems like everything is stacked against them."

How is newsgathering likely to change by 2025?
Natalie: "I can see more collaboration between titles and news organisations. Pooling resources and using that voice to make a change in the regions."

Maisha: "There will be a dominance of online reporting which could be less objective and less probing because of fewer resources. There will be more humdrum, data-led news items."

Tom: "Local print media will be on its last legs in all but the biggest cities. I think social media, and Facebook in particular, will grow as the key channels for a small business to get the news out, direct to the community and potential customers. This will also help them get picked up by the media. Even granny and grandpa will read their paper on an iPad – but this doesn't mean the core elements of good news stories will change."

Beermat PR Lesson #5
Think like a journalist

7. Getting your Press Release right

The press release is still the best way to get news out to a wide range of media outlets.

Think of this as the persuasive pitch you will use to convince the editor to like your story. Don't think of it as the finished article and then get upset when it isn't published just as you wrote it. That's not what happens. Or at least, not what should happen. Natalie Fahy, the editor at the Nottingham Post, says: "Don't be overly precious about copy and quotes. You need to trust the journalist. We won't come back to you if you want to edit everything because we don't have time for that. Of course, if you're not happy we'll work to resolve that."

Preparing your press release
Here are some tips for making a good press release.

#Tip 1: Cover the facts in the first paragraph: answering the who, what, why, when, where, and how questions the reader needs. If space is short, this might be all the editor can use, but at least the key information is there for them to include.

#Tip 2: The second and third paragraphs should build on the first and carry any significant details.

#Tip 3: Include a quote: this adds personality and endorsement to the story. The person quoted is usually the one who is willing to be interviewed – so if not you, make sure the person is comfortable about this.

#Tip 4: Use 1.5 line-spacing, wide margins, and type **ENDS** to indicate you have finished.

#Tip 5: Use notes under the release text to carry useful background information that reporters can use for research.

#Tip 6: Choose a simple but attention-grabbing title that reinforces the overall message. Don't try to be clever and craft the final headline. That's the job of the sub-editor.

#Tip 7: Type **PRESS RELEASE** at the top, date it, and indicate a time when the information can be published. This is particularly important if for some reason you need the news to be embargoed. You may want to time an announcement to be sure that all staff have been informed of a major company decision before it is made public. You provide the news to the media on the professional understanding that they will respect the embargo. However, naming no names, I have been let down by headline-grabbing editors who wanted to break the news early. Not good for professional relations. What did I say about respect for each other's jobs?

#Tip 8: Limit your release to four or five paragraphs at the most. Short, informative, and interesting goes down well with busy reporters. No superlatives. No exclamation marks.

#Tip 9: Do you have a photo? Make sure it is taken in landscape and is high resolution (300dpi) and at least 1MB.

#Tip 10: Proofread your release before it goes out. Then get someone else to do it again. It's amazzing what you can misss......

Sending it
You've hit full stop for the final time. You've proofread. You're happy. You've checked it with anyone mentioned or quoted. Your press release is ready to be sent out.

Now, where do you send it? You'll need to build a list of media contacts and you should find out as much as you can about how they work. When are they most likely to be planning their content and how do they like to be contacted?

Do your research thoroughly. As editor of a national journal for business advisers, I was frequently contacted by potential contributors or their PR representatives who wanted me to carry their articles. I could immediately spot those who were familiar with the publication and had thought about the needs of the readers. It made my decision to run an item much easier, and I also felt that I could trust them to deliver what I needed on time, too.

Is there a perfect time to send my news? Most of us in the PR industry would agree that earlier in the week is the best time to send out news – probably Tuesday or Wednesday. Just check copy deadlines if you are aiming for print magazines and weekend editions.

However, most small businesses and freelancers are not generating ground-breaking or urgent news stories – but if you do, frankly any time of the day or night is right to contact the media. That said, if it warrants 'urgent' they are probably chasing you for the story and you might need some crisis-handling advice. More on that later.

So how should you send the news? We have come a long way from the days of my early career when I'd type the press release, print 100 or so copies, stick them in envelopes, stamp, and post. But it worked, and we still got return calls from editors and coverage for clients.

It's all very different now and a whole lot easier.

I asked my journalist colleagues how they like to be contacted. All said by email at first, unless you already know them, in which case a call if it's in response to a request, or a breaking news item.

"Scanning an email provides a way of quickly assessing whether the item is relevant," says Daily Express business and personal finance reporter, Maisha Frost. That way, she can quickly decide whether the item is relevant.

Daily Mail's Tom Witherow provides an example of what that email pitch should ideally look like. His key message is that the email must be brief, include key points but also be persuasive about why it is something that the publication would like to cover. Tell the journalist what you're able to offer, the time frame and how to get in touch.

Subject Line
Birkenhead salon does 1,000 haircuts in 24 hours for charity.

Dear Tom,
I'm emailing with a news idea [for your business page] about … … …I have come to you first with this because I think it works well for your reader. It is [a feel-good local news story], [a new angle of an important local issue], [etc]. I thought it was relevant for your publication because of your excellent coverage of [a couple of recent news stories on this subject that have been well read].

The opening sentence
A hairdresser in Birkenhead has raised £12,000 for charity by cutting 1,000 heads of hair in 24 hours – including [local celeb/ the mayor].

The Key Facts:
Four members of staff cut xx heads of hair per hour for 24 hours to reach the target.

We undertook the challenge because of [connection to charity]

I can also offer you a full set of photos, a phone interview at a convenient time today or tomorrow, and I can make time for posed photos, a radio interview or filming. I can also help you with contacts to help with quotes for the story.

I have included the full press release below, but please don't hesitate to contact me if you need further information. To help with the timescale, I am looking to place this article this week/in the next couple of days.
I look forward to hearing from you,
XX
[Phone numbers/email address/social media handles]

The all-important follow-up

Given that busy journalists receive hundreds of press releases a day, you've still got some work to do to get it seen.

If you are doing your own PR or, like me, being paid by a client to get some coverage for them, the pressure is on to follow the press release with either a call, email, or private message on social media.

Ideally, try to send your release to a specific person. If you call the switchboard not knowing who to ask for, you'll get passed around the various news desks repeating your story – a waste of effort and highly dispiriting.

After 25 years in the PR business, here is what I do (and I will allow my journalist colleagues to disagree with me):

1. Unless your news needs urgent attention, wait a day or so before getting in touch.
2. Forward the original press release email to individual contacts, asking them to check that it has been received.
3. No response, then call. I tend to limit this to between 11 am and 3 pm, which avoids morning editorial planning meetings or late afternoon deadlines. No, the 24/7 media machine doesn't have

deadlines in the way it used to. But as Richard Tyler, editor of The Times Enterprise Network, says: "There are bad times of the day to call. Avoid 4 pm onwards, when people are likely to be trying to concentrate on writing a story that must be filed to a news desk in the next five minutes! Other media will differ – the basic rule of thumb will be the nearer you call to their deadline the more stressed they will be."

4. Beware of calling a local radio station either on the hour or half-hour. The person who answers may be about to go on-air with the news headlines.
5. The phone call response is most likely to be "we'll be in touch if we like your item" or "if you haven't already heard from us, I doubt we're covering it". Brutal, but honest.
6. Don't be put off if you don't succeed: ask why, as the answer could be very useful and help you in the future (even if it reveals that some journalists base their decisions on rubbish reasons). Remember journalists move on and what may not suit one, may be perfect for another. Equally an idea that has no legs at one moment in time then assumes enormous significance just a few weeks later. Journalists remember helpful contacts and tend to keep in touch – so the next time they want a comment or a business to feature at short notice make sure yours is the number they call.
7. Then again, let's assume the person on the other end asks you to explain what it's about. You have a few seconds to get the basic facts covered before time's up. Often, the news desk is interested and asks you to send the release again (this time to them personally) because it has genuinely not been spotted and has potential.
8. Have a fact file of information about your business and a set of professionally taken photographs ready to go. And be available at a moment's notice for interviews or responding to quick fact check questions by text. I know this isn't always possible as busy business owners – but deadlines mean opportunities can be lost by not being responsive.

If you are not confident about talking to editors, you could try getting in touch with freelance writers. Regular reading of any trade or local paper will show how the same people are filing stories. Especially if they specialise in a particular industry. Can you get to know them? Find them on Twitter and follow their posts and conversations. They may be in a better position to help by telling you if your story is as strong as you think. If they like it, they will write it up and sell it into your target publication themselves.

Look out for requests on Twitter #journorequest and visit the web service helpareporter.com. Many freelancers hang out here.

8. Yikes! I'm being Interviewed!

Right. You've put your head above the parapet and contacted your target media using a press release. Now, one possible – and very positive – outcome would be a chance to do an interview on radio or TV.

Great. Nothing like the thought of being in front of a camera or microphone to get the heart pumping. What happens next? Your mind goes blank.

Please don't go into a media interview unprepared. Whether novice or professional, that's a recipe for disaster. Preparation is crucial, so I've asked former ITV presenter and founder of PLC Media, Dan Baker, to give us some advice.

Question: I'm a small business owner with a news story that has just got picked up by local radio. I had sent them a press release and now I'm suddenly confronted with interest. What should I consider before I agree to do the interview? What questions should I ask the person who has just called me?

Answer: First things first: if you've sent out a press release and attracted attention from the media – well done! That is a great achievement.

So, what to consider? If you sent your news to that media contact then presumably it's an outlet you wanted coverage from. It would be a bit odd if you now decided not to do an interview.

Ask them some fundamental questions: is it being broadcast live, or is it being pre-recorded; how much do you want from me; will you just be interviewing me on this story; what sort of angle or direction do you plan to take?

Don't bother asking for a list of questions, tempting though it is. It's a poor reporter that has a list of questions – we're 'active listeners': in other words, our second question is (or at least should be) motivated by your first response. Talk through logistics too. Be comfortable with asking where the interview will take place (studio or phone) and when.

Question: So, I've decided to go ahead. How should I prepare for a radio interview?

Answer: Think about what it is you want to say. Don't get bogged down with "I wonder what they'll ask me", because who knows what they'll ask? They probably don't! Turn the telescope round: if you were listening to an interview on this subject, what would you find interesting, engaging, or impactful?

Think about the language you'll use. Don't use jargon, don't over-formalise what you're planning to say – keep things simple. And practise what you're planning to say as well, just as you would with a presentation. Make sure the first time you say out loud what you want to say isn't when there's a microphone in your face or a reporter at the other end of the phone. Get comfortable with the messaging and the language well in advance.

If it's a contentious issue, and if it's something that's coming up in the future, rather than on that day, think about bringing in a media trainer who will talk this all through in a lot more detail and then give you a chance to do some dummy-run interviews.

Question: That's great, Dan, but I'm sure to be nervous. I don't want to freeze. What can I do to avoid this happening, even though I know it's being recorded?

Answer: Harness the adrenalin. A few nerves are fine – it's people who don't feel any nerves at all who tend to be a bit of a loose cannon. Working out what you want to say and how you want to say it, practising it, bouncing it around with colleagues or even friends and family will help. And if it's recorded, it doesn't matter if you get a bit of brain freeze because it's not live and any glitches will be edited out. Just ask them to repeat the question and have another go.

Question: How can I be sure the best bits aren't edited out?

Answer: You can't! Edited interviews are deceptively difficult to control. Yes, it may feel safer to do something edited rather than going live, but you lose a large degree of control straight away as it's likely only a chunk will ever see the light of day, and the reporter chooses that chunk. If you get a choice, always opt for a live interview as it's much easier to control the ultimate output. The trick with an edited interview is to work those key messages and ideas into every single answer – subtly, but consistently. That's the only way to make sure that what you're there to say isn't edited out. I admit it's tough to do, but it's what experienced interviewees have been trained to do.

Question: The local TV station also likes my story and insists they need to film today. Do I just agree, or can I ask for time and location changes?

Answer: Great news – a bit of TV coverage will open your story up to a much bigger audience. You can, within reason, dictate where the interview takes place. And in terms of time, yes, it needs to be a time that works for you. That said, if it's been on the radio that day, it will need to be the same day for TV: they won't want to cover it tomorrow as by then it's considered yesterday's news. It really needs to be before 3 pm to give the reporter time to get the story edited. The broadcast media news cycle is fast-moving and if you miss it, you're very unlikely to get a second chance.

Question: How do I stay calm for the camera?

Answer: Just remember, live is the best option because, other than the questions, there is no editorial intervention. People see and hear what you say, as you say it. So, keep calm, stick to your messaging, keep things simple. The more complicated you make things, the more anxious you'll get and the less impact you'll have. Most local news reports last around two to three minutes maximum, including the introduction. In a live TV interview you probably only have a maximum of two minutes of screen time. If it's a soundbite, it's more likely to be 15 seconds. Another reason why 'live' is best.

Try visualising someone on the other side of the camera, preferably someone you like, and talk to them. I always used to imagine I was talking to my mum or dad: in fact, they were usually watching me anyway. That helped to bring down my nerves and to warm up my performance.

Dan's advice is confirmed by the journalists I contacted. They added:
- "Just be yourself, because we can tell if you are not."
- "Speak from the heart about your business and be passionate."
- "The journalist's job is to ask the questions that get the best answers. Just make sure you have examples of work done and clients helped, not just flat statements of fact."
- "Don't be afraid to give information about your business, and biographical details about yourself. It is the variety of details and information that makes the story unique."

9. Creating your Own Content

The business of earning space in established media is becoming ever more subverted by 'owned and shared' publicity: noise that you make for yourself. In effect, you can become your own reporter by blogging and vlogging.

The trick is to think like a journalist, and to write, film, and record like a journalist. Consider what your audience wants or needs from your content, not just what you want to say. 'Look at me' content doesn't do much for your reputation. It is incredibly tedious.

Blogging

One of the most useful and popular ways to demonstrate your expertise, insights, and your core values too, is to write a blog. You're not restricted to a certain style; in fact, you should adjust your tone and approach to suit different audiences, just as you would in conversation. You don't have to worry about the word count but given our tendency to short attention spans I suggest a three-to-four-minute read is ideal. That's around 500 words.

You can write and post as frequently as you wish. There are no deadlines, apart from the ones you set yourself, of course. Simple.

Alpkit's publicity relies mostly on this sort of content marketing. The company shares stories of adventures, supported by suggestions for outdoor clothing and equipment. They also have a band of ambassadors whose careers and aspirations they actively support. This generates a wealth of human-interest stories aligned with the company's core values and products.

If you already write a blog or are thinking about starting one, here are a few ideas to get you started.

- **Problem-solving or how-to guides**. Most businesses receive the same queries repeatedly. Your blog post will help a myriad of potential customers and show you in a good, helpful light.
- **Evergreen.** A follow-on from this first point is to identify timeless content that you can write about and will never be outdated. As I've found after 25 years in the business, there are unchanging principles of PR which merit repetition.
- **Thought leadership**. Is there something happening in your industry that you want to comment on? Your blog is the best place to do it.
- **Company insight.** Are you working on something cool that you want to describe and share with your audience? Then you should – if it's not a company secret. Just think about what would make this insight genuinely interesting for them.

The best thing about blogs is that you own the content and can publish it in your own time. It allows you to use your own photos and videos and to construct the content you want. A good blog is also a PR expert's dream. If your articles are well written and topical, then any public relations professional you might eventually employ will be able to repurpose the content and offer it to be published in relevant publications. A real win-win situation.

There is a downside. How do you find the time to write a regular blog alongside your busy day-to-day work? Running a popular blog is time-consuming, but as your business grows and you take on staff, the writing can be done by others. This way your posts benefit from having a mix of different writing styles, different topics, and varying content. Plus, your colleagues get to demonstrate their expertise too.

Vlogging

Vlogging is a very similar exercise to blogging… you just don't do any writing, other than providing yourself with some kind of script or bullets.

Instead, it is all about speaking into a camera and creating a video. The biggest benefit of vlogging is that it allows you to connect with your audience in real-time and is particularly useful when it comes to virtual demonstrations.

Why should you consider vlogging for your business? Cision, the multinational tech company, reckons that by 2023, 82 per cent of all content on the web will be video based: a truly remarkable prediction.

Case study

How vlogging can be a key tool for engaging your audience

There's no doubt about it, COVID-19 forced many businesses to think differently.

One such business was Daltons Wadkin. Based in Nottingham, the business is one of the UK's longest-established distributors and manufacturers of industrial woodworking machinery. However, after returning to the office in May 2020, they needed to come up with a new way of connecting with their customers and clients who didn't feel safe travelling to their showroom.

This is where vlogging and virtual demonstrations came in handy.

While Daltons Wadkin already had a YouTube channel where they uploaded generic content, the business tapped into the Zoom-hype to hold organised and live one-to-one demonstrations with their clients, allowing them to explore the benefits of their machinery and answer specific questions.

> Alex Dalton, director of Daltons Wadkin, said: "While it is still possible to discuss sales or queries over the phone, in our experience, there's nothing quite like talking them over in person.
>
> "That's why video is going to become an increasingly important tool for businesses like ours. Audiences feel far more engaged with what you are demonstrating if they see a person talking to them.
>
> "We have one guy on camera who is always muted; the demonstrator wears a microphone and is audio-only and then we also have the attending customer, which could be one person or even several, on screen.
>
> "The biggest benefit, of course, is that this medium allows us to engage with our customer base about a product, service, or application, no matter where they are in the UK.
>
> "We see it as a big part of the consumer journey. It gives customers the chance to make sure the particular equipment we are talking about is suitable for their requirements and covers a lot of the groundwork before either party commits time and travel to complete the sales process."

The positives of vlogging are clear. It saves valuable time. Virtual demonstrations can be held in real-time. It doesn't take a lot of effort. It allows you to connect with your customer base, no matter where they are located.

Daltons Wadkin has a YouTube channel and this has been a great way for the business to upload generic content, largely based on the type of user queries they receive from potential customers.

Once uploaded, it's yours to own and is a great way of creating conversations with your customers and driving them to your website, which should always be your end goal when producing this type of content.

A word of caution. A truly cringe-worthy piece of video might damage your reputation. If you are not confident with the camera, you probably need help. I turned for advice to Jack Delaney, founder of the video production company, Simply Thrilled. I asked him a few questions:

Question: I'm going to try and use my own equipment to make a video, so what will I need?

Answer: If you are looking to create a set of testimonials, your smartphone will do. Film in landscape for YouTube and portrait for Instagram. Your next option is to use a DSLR camera, as most have a video mode. I'd recommend using a stabiliser or tripod, so shots avoid the amateur shakes. When it comes to editing, you'll find iMovie easy to use. The more sophisticated programmes like Adobe Premiere or Final Cut Pro will come with a monthly charge.

Question: How do I prepare for filming?

Answer: You should have a list of all the shots you want to capture on filming days. Once you've done the chronological order of the finished film, make a second list which is the best logistical order to film in. So, for instance, if you want the top and the tail of a piece to be at the same location, think about filming them both at the same time. Ask talent (that's anyone being filmed) to wear clothes without logos or close-together lines, which interfere with the camera. Writing a script is helpful too – this doesn't need to be a precise affair; it can just be talking points.

Question: Any legal things to consider?

Answer: Most local councils will allow you to film in crews of five or less if you don't get in anyone's way. However, in some places like the London

Borough of Westminster you need permission to have a camera on a tripod. Just check beforehand.

If you are using your video for commercial purposes, you should ask the people you are filming to fill out a permissions form. This allows you to release images of them. Please make sure permission is given to film youngsters under the age of 16, and it might be wise for them to have a chaperone. Just check first.

Question: What common mistakes do amateurs make?

Answer: Mistake number one must be moving the camera whilst recording the shot. Someone's speaking – giving a testimonial for your wonderful services – and you move in on their face or try for a different angle... No! If you want to mix up the shots, record once without moving the camera and then record again from a different angle. Then edit.

Mistake number two is that nobody thinks about sound quality until it's too late. Our ears are designed to pick up sounds we want to hear (someone's voice, for instance) and dialling down the other noises (rain falling outside, a kettle boiling in a nearby room, etc). Microphones are not. If you're using a camera mic, move closer to the subject (what we would call a close-up shot). Always film out of the wind (enemy number one) and where there are fewer passers-by or other ambient noise, which can sound like an earthquake on video.

You can find loads of online tutorials covering things like lighting, white balance, exposure, and focus.

Question: OK, so I realise I need to hire a filmmaker. How much should I budget?

Answer: That will depend on the complexity of the finished item. Production can start around the low four figures, while commercial productions, such as the John Lewis Christmas advert, cost into the millions. Be clear about what you're hoping to achieve: what purpose the video serves in your marketing and communications mix. If you're short on pennies, a professional filmmaker will suggest affordable alternatives.

Jack can be found at simply-thrilled.com

David Hanney of Alpkit tells me that they made several films about individuals, which they called Mountain Journal Shorts. Although they made them for themselves, the videos ended up at film festivals, on Channel 4 and the most successful, *Chasing the Sublime*, ran on the Oprah Show in the US. Amazing how a small UK brand based in Derbyshire achieved such international coverage.

Podcasts

While the statistics for people listening to radio each week are impressive, equally so is the number tuning into podcasts. In 2020, 7.1 million people reportedly listened to podcasts each week.

Unlike local radio stations, which cover numerous topics, podcasts are best tailored and dedicated to specific sectors and talking points. Take some time to find out which podcasts cover your industry, how regular they are, what content they discuss, and then ask if you can be interviewed. Although a podcast's listener base will be smaller, its focus means that you are more than likely to be speaking directly to your target audience and potential customers by making an appearance.

If the popular, professionalised podcasts run by industry influencers don't want you as a guest, why not record your own? The costs of set-up, recording, and editing are well within an amateur's budget. The key is in the planning. You'll need to record in a space with good acoustics (fewer surfaces like windows and mirrors and preferably carpeted). Editing software online is easy to find and use. Just practise, practise, and practise until you are happy with the quality. Find a graphic or photo to illustrate the theme and post it on your social media channels. Who knows? You might become the next industry influencer.

Newsjacking

Newsjacking is the art of adding your thoughts and views into breaking news stories or features and piggybacking off topical news trends to get you or your brand noticed. It is a growing trend in PR. You provide extra details, comments, or opinions on a piece and the journalists spot your interest. While bigger PR agencies have the capabilities to act as a business' dedicated newsroom and track specific news items that are ideal for you, this is a practice you can do yourself.

Use the hashtag *#JournoRequest* on Twitter to see the latest comments and views from journalists looking for help on a current topic. Requests range across all trade, local, regional, and even national publications, and opportunities pop up daily.

While this process often involves writing, there are many requests from journalists looking to speak directly with an industry expert like you. Remember what Dan and I said earlier about media training and getting ready to be the industry pundit. Go in primed and ready.

Be quick, though! As soon as these opportunities arise, savvy PR professionals will jump in to pitch their clients. So, if you know there is a breaking news story coming up in your industry, get your views written down. When the requests start to flow on Twitter, you will be primed and ready to add your thoughts and secure interviews. Hardy news perennials include the Budget, poverty and homelessness, house prices, and employment statistics.

Visual content

As the saying goes: *a picture is worth a thousand words.* That's why it's so important to provide a strong photo to go with your news pieces and to provide visual content for your website, social media channels, and email marketing. For the record, when we refer to visual content, we're talking about photos, graphics, and video.

Does it really make that much of an impact? Well yes, it does.

Let's take Facebook as an example. After analysing 8,000 posts across B2B and B2C businesses, HubSpot reported that content including some form of visual had 53 per cent more likes and 104 per cent more comments than those that didn't. Other researchers support this finding. One of the world's top social media strategists, Jeff Bullas, discovered that Facebook posts with photos received, on average, a 37 per cent increase in engagement. We're talking incredible numbers here. The trend is similar for Twitter, too, which, alongside Facebook and Instagram, should be considered an important audience-reaching tool for your business.

The fact is we humans don't want to be looking at long streams of text. Our eyes are drawn to colour, people, products, imagination, and creativity. In a world dominated by the internet, your online presence should not be any different.

Want another impressive stat? Did you know that we only recall 10 per cent of what we hear in a presentation? But if you pair a relevant image with your message, we can recall 65 per cent of the information after three days. Amazing how the brain works!

Here are just a few easy tips and tricks to help you add visual content to your business:

- **Organic.** The best way to stand out is by being original. Take photos that no one else could. Your business is yours to own, so show it off in the best possible light
- **Make the most of free websites.** Royalty-free sites, like Unsplash and Pixelbay, allow you to download and use photos for free. There are also free video-editing websites to try out if you're feeling a little creative.
- **Pay a professional photographer.** This is best done once your business is starting to gather some momentum. Provide the photographer with a brief and they will be able to produce a batch of photos (150–200 over a two-hour session) that represent your business in the best possible way. It's fine taking your own, but there's no doubt a professional shot is worth the investment. Budget between £75 and £150 per hour, but a lot depends on whether studio hire is needed too.
- **Share content.** Depending on your industry, you may be able to share visual content created by your customers or audience. This is a real win-win situation. Your audience is shouting about your product and you get to share great content out of it.
- **Create your own graphics.** Like hiring a professional photographer, this is more for the established business that may be lucky enough to have a graphic designer on site. If that's the case, make use of them. Infographics and GIFs are proven champions for social media engagement.

A word of caution. Don't come across in your images as unaware. Consider the context and situation. I am writing this at the height of the COVID-19 pandemic so at the moment you don't want to be posting images of people not adhering to the social distancing and hygiene rules and regulations. Visual content, misapplied, is a sure-fire way of attracting the wrong kind of attention.

Newsletters

I don't receive many printed corporate newsletters anymore, but I do value printed communications from the charities I support. If you happen to be handling PR for a charity, you and your marketing colleagues will probably put a serious budget into a regular newsletter.

This may reflect the slightly older demographic of your donors so keep up the good work producing hardcopy newsletters. You'll probably be keeping in touch with Gen X, Y, and Z on Instagram and TikTok.

The same writing principles should apply to your newsletters, online, and in print, as to all your communications.

Adopt the mindset and reporting style of a journalist and consider the reader and their interests. Design your content magazine-style:

- present your news but emphasise how this will affect the reader
- give your views or advice on recent changes to legislation
- ask a member of staff to review a newly published book chosen to suit readers. General management titles work well.
- announce your company's latest charitable effort, with an accompanying photo of the staff team on the summit of Kilimanjaro.

It's amazing how a skilful corporate writer can weave your messages into such items and leave the reader wanting to get in touch with you or feel good about buying from you. You are literally creating your own editorial coverage. Above all, use story-telling techniques that never fail to get attention and stick in the mind. I'd recommend a read of John Yorke's book *Into the Woods* (Penguin) if you want to explore the principles behind storytelling in more depth.

Take a look at the newsletters you receive. Which ones do you read, and which do you bin or delete? Ask yourself why. The answer will probably be whether it is of use to you. Then be ruthless next time you plan and write your own.

> **Beermat PR Lesson #6**
> *Blow your own trumpet –*
> *but make sure it's pleasant for the listener*

10. Networking

I should say a few words about business networking. It does come under PR because, well used, it can add to your reputation-building and make others aware of your existence, which, as you must have gathered by now, is what PR is all about.

At its simplest, business networking refers to the building and cultivating of relationships with people of similar interests in ways that can benefit everyone. Why is it so important for smaller businesses? Because it's about creating relationships with others that should help to expand your business' ability to find new customers, to potentially collaborate, and grow. A key result of effective networking is to make you known. Please, please note: networking is not, and was never meant to be a sales attack.

There are plenty of businesspeople I know who loathe organised business networking events with a passion. Why is this? What have we done to make such a natural human behaviour and valuable component of the business toolkit so unfathomably frightful? After all, most of us think nothing of meeting up with a few friends – and their friends – in a social setting (current COVID-19 restrictions permitting), having a good chat, and getting to know them.

I asked around for some opinions. Boy, did I get some! The only polite word to describe the worst networking events is 'beige'. Beige surroundings, beige food, beige speakers, and beige attire. It sounds as though we need a radical campaign to rescue this valuable activity from those who have buried the true value in – well – beigeness.

Let's bring it back to what it was always meant to achieve: building relationships founded on understanding the other person and willingness to help them and to see this as a long-term ambition. Business networking and the art of getting to know someone is a marathon, not a sprint. A long and happy marriage, not the equivalent of speed-dating.

We heard earlier from the author, Ladey Adey. In her latest book, *Successful Business Networking Online*, she uncovers the dos and don'ts of online networking, especially now that so many encounters are taking place on tech platforms like Zoom and Microsoft Teams. Lockdown restrictions have at least done away with the beige location. We learn so much about our onscreen friends by seeing their study, dining room, or kitchen surroundings, not to mention the family members and pets who stray into view. You can bring your own food, choose from a global programme of speakers and topics, and wear whatever colourful top or bottoms you like. It seems that the COVID-19 pandemic has done away with the 'beige' and gone some way to re-energising our connection with others in business, albeit on screen.

To help you decide which networks to join, here are three tests you can apply, whether you are meeting face-to-face or online.

1. Does the organiser or host actively introduce members and look for ways to connect you to others? An effective networking group finds ways to remain in touch beyond the regular formal meetings, perhaps in special interest groups. I only belong to one such organisation, which has become my extended business family. This is Catena (Latin for 'chain' or 'link'). Its owner, Claire Bicknell, is proactive in making introductions and spotting business connections that may help people. She organises Sector Interest Group meetings where we discuss issues in greater depth and, as a result, learn more about each other's knowledge and experience.

   Check them out at catena-business-network.com.

2. Are the formal gatherings innovative, informative, and fun? Doing something together like a round of golf, watching a cricket match, or learning from a wine tasting expert gets people talking – and hopefully laughing too. I like the idea of 'Net-Walking', taking a long hike across the hills with plenty of opportunities to chat and then enjoy a pub meal afterwards.

3. Does the network attract members who believe in the *'marathon-not-a-sprint'* principle? Members who just 'get it'. If you choose your business networks along these lines, you are much more likely to enjoy the time spent with other business owners who you can learn from, or possibly eventually work with.

11. Digital PR – Maximise and Measure

Throughout the book, I've tried to interweave what might be termed traditional PR and digital PR. The two should work together, delivering the overall aims of your communications campaigns in their own special ways. However, the world of digital PR has become much more technical. As a novice, you would be pushed to deliver the same kind of results achieved by specialist agencies such as Hallam, where my two co-writers work.

But there are things you can do. So, over to you, Tom and Rebecca.

The aim of social media is twofold. It needs to be fun and engaging, but it also needs to drive your audience to your website. Don't miss a trick by forgetting to include your website in your profile biography wherever it appears. Ensure it is one of the first things your audience will see when they click through to your social media channels. Likewise, your website should contain links to all your social media profiles.

Do you want to rank higher on Google than your competitors? Do you want to increase the amount of traffic to your website? One of the biggest ranking factors that Google takes into consideration is the number of quality backlinks to your site.

What are backlinks? Simply put, it is when another website links to yours, either via a page or by publishing one of your articles. Quality is essential here. You want to get links from sites that have a high-ranking authority, otherwise known as domain ranking, or "DR" if you want to sound smart. To get a backlink, you need to provide external sites with content that gives them a reason to link back to you.

Domain rankings are between 0 and 100. The higher the number, the better its authority. Speaking from a digital PR professional's point of view, getting content on these sites to get a backlink is the holy grail if ranking highly on Google's search results is the name of the game for your business. Typical content might include a strong press release, a piece of research, a feature article, or an interview.

Do not fall into the trap of paying for low-quality links. Google wants its users to be fed highly relevant material and can penalise brands that pay for poor links. You want people to choose to visit your site because they enjoy what you have to offer.

How can I get links to my site?
You can generate manual links back to your website using directories and getting partner links, but this will only get you so far. Which websites have the highest authority? News sites! And how do you get links to your site from a news site? By getting a news story placed. So, by combining traditional PR and digital PR, you'll gain brand awareness, while also increasing your chances of ranking higher on Google and other search engines.

Here are some other ways you can generate backlinks to your site.

Demonstrate your thought leadership
We covered this earlier in the book: it's about offering your industry expertise to publications through well-written articles or blogs. Got an opinion on the future of your industry? Want to discuss new and upcoming trends? What about the latest regulation in your sector? People like opinions, and publications like publishing what people think. If you can draft an opinion piece, or advice article, into an 800-word blog, send it to a trade magazine that has a relevant audience. Chances are that the publication will publish and give you a link back – and you'll get brand exposure.

Use your partners

Have you worked with local councils, charities, or other organisations? If so, here is a great opportunity to gain a link back to your website. Many sites have a 'partners' section, where they list, and link to, the partners they work with. Go ahead and link to your current partners on your site too and invite them to do the same. If the partnership is notable, consider a joint announcement in a press release to gain extra coverage and brand recognition.

Add your company to business directories

This is a more manual job than the others. Many websites, including regional news sites, have business directories on their site. If you search for directories in your area and your sector, hundreds will come up. However, some directories can be quite spammy, so as a rule – if it looks dodgy, it probably is. Steer clear. As a starting point, fill out the directory form on the relevant business pages in your local paper. This will be a free way to get listed and secure backlinks from recognised and reliable sites.

Other routes to strong digital PR

Run a competition

People love freebies and what better way to give something away than by running a competition? It doesn't have to be a difficult challenge either. You could keep it as simple as encouraging your audience to like and share a post on your social media, or to comment by tagging in a friend and family member. This is an easy way to spread your business' name in a very short space of time.

Post an event

Thinking of planning an event? If so, a social media channel like Facebook allows you to create a dedicated page to raise awareness with your online community. Then you will be able to track interest, share information, post images and videos, and answer any queries before or after the event has taken place.

Point to your website
The aim of social media is two-fold. First, posts should be fun and engaging, but they also need to drive your audience to your website. Don't miss a trick by forgetting to include your domain link in your profile biography wherever it appears. It is one of the first things your audience will see when they click through to your social channel. Second, your website should contain links to all your social profiles. Make time to update your website regularly.

Interaction
Yes, you are entertaining a wide audience, but each one of your followers wants to see and feel that personal touch. Use your social media channels to talk to them, maybe answering questions, sharing their content about your business, or running polls to get their thoughts. Connect emotionally too. Show them you care and can solve a problem they have.

Alumni stories
Did you, or one of your employees, graduate from a university or notable college? Well, you're in luck because universities adore alumni success stories, and may run them – with links to your site, of course.

If you have started your own company, they will probably be interested in how you did it and include a feature about you on their website. It is also quality content and promotion for their institution. So, email the alumni contact at the university you went to, and offer your story. Loughborough University spotted Andrew Walker's start-up and the award wins for TEA REX and featured him on the alumni pages.

Louise tells us that she graduated from the University of Newcastle-upon-Tyne in 1983. She heard nothing from the institution for nearly 30 years. Then in 2016, the alumni office spotted that she had received an honour. Before long, Louise was being interviewed and was asked to provide a picture in her posh hat outside Buckingham Palace. Then she received several LinkedIn requests from fellow Newcastle graduates who, 40 years on, are now part of her business network. Staying in touch with your former place of learning has never been easier and means you can tell them what you are doing – and all about those awards you've won, too.

How do I measure my digital PR results?
Before even starting on any piece of content for your digital PR, ask yourself what you want to achieve. What would success look like? Embarking on a digital PR campaign without a method for evaluating results is like playing darts in a pitch-black room. You might think you have aimed well and done everything right, but you'll never be sure whether you hit the bullseye, or even the board, until you turn the lights back on.

Here are five indicators of a campaign's effectiveness.

A rise in your domain ranking
As we mentioned earlier, domain ranking, DR, is how Google sees your website. Think of it as a credit score. It is a number – typically out of 100 – that determines how authoritative your website is. You can get a free domain rating by Googling 'Ahrefs Free Backlink Checker'. The higher your rank, the higher up Google's search results you are.

A rise in published links
"We would love to run your article and of course we will include that link." These words are music to every digital PR professional's ears. One of the easiest ways to track how successful your article or campaign has been is to count the number of times it has been published – something that can be achieved very easily by doing a quick Google search in the *news* section. This can be found at the top of a Google search, alongside images, shopping, videos, and more.

A bonus of this, or course, is the relationship you have built with a reporter or editor who might come back to you for a later comment or article.

An increase in the number of page views

Maybe you have a particular product that hasn't been selling so well on your website recently. Or maybe you have a service page that you want your audience to see. If this is the case, it's time to sit down and brainstorm creative ways you can get it in front of your audience.

If you can create a story that is placed on a landing page on your website which engages with the press, it's also likely to engage your target audience. This story could be a piece of research, a video, an infographic, or a prediction piece. A link from the press site will see traffic from people clicking through to your website, potentially leading to more sales. And if you share the story on your social media, other people will choose to visit your site.

There are free tools on the web that will help you see how your website is performing and how much attention it is attracting. *Exposure Ninja* and *Google Analytics* are two examples that can show these results, while *SEMRush's All-in-one Marketing Toolkit* is an industry-wide popular tool for checking how much traffic a website gets. Why not use a seven-day trial to see what it is all about?

A longer page linger

"Stick around a little longer…" The main goal of any website is to keep people hooked for as long as possible. Eye-catching, long-form content (between 700 and 2,000 words) and informative articles are one of the best-known ways of achieving this. Tools like the ones mentioned will give you the average time a customer is spending on your website.

An increase in social media attention

Generally, this can be measured in the number of likes, comments, shares, or views a specific piece of content has received. The better the performance, the higher the reach and the potential for more people to view and interact with you. There are two primary ways to find out how many social media shares your content has gained.

- You can search manually on Twitter, LinkedIn, and Facebook, by copying and pasting in the headline or the URL.

- You can use your one free link a day on *BuzzSumo.com*. This allows you to paste the link of your blog into its search function and then tells you the number of shares, likes, and engagements on Facebook, Twitter, Pinterest, and Reddit.

So, get uploading items to your website, and post about them on your social media, to make sure your direct audience knows what you are talking about.

In this digital-first world, it's important to take new media seriously. Maximise and measure your digital PR efforts so that the all-important search finds you first.

Beermat PR Lesson #7
Get digitally savvy

---

12. Skills for DIY PR

Well done. You've made it this far. I hope you don't feel overwhelmed by the amount of work involved in doing PR for you and your business. If it helps, here are a few of the skills you would find useful. Don't let it put you off having a go at your own PR as I have yet to come across a public relations professional who gets anywhere near exhibiting all these skills.

Invest in some training if necessary. Arm yourself to go into battle.

Strategic Thinking
If you already run your own business, then I reckon you already have an element of strategic thinker in you. You got home from your summer break, looked in the mirror, and said to yourself: "I want a change." Rung one on the strategic thinking ladder. Rung two: "I have an idea for a business and think it will give me the change and the success I want." And so on, up the strategic thinking ladder until you reach the top and can see the bigger picture. Don't allow too much detail to get in the way – from a PR perspective, you are gazing at the profile and reputation you aspire to in five years' time.

Planning
If you learn one thing from this book, make it 'Plan First: Then Act Second'. Planning takes discipline and thoroughness. If you are the kind of person who likes making lists, keeps a regular diary, books your holidays early and remembers birthdays, you will probably be well suited to PR campaign planning. You like lists.

It's the bit I enjoy most. Drilling into the detail of messaging, target audience analysis, and the communications channels to bring them together. Schedule your news and writing tasks month by month, and devise ways to create headlines through social media postings. Then, once completed, you'll get to tick them off the to-do list. One by one. It's very satisfying.

Creativity

Yet PR is also a creative, imaginative activity. Most people are more creative than they think, but if this is not you – try it first, you may be surprised – then admit defeat and outsource it to one of the many creative types who have made a profession of PR.

Here's an example of creative PR from a piece of work I did for the former Society for Editors and Proofreaders (SfEP), now the Chartered Institute of Editing and Proofreading. Much of our work with them was rather dry, but one Christmas we came up with a light-hearted but topical and timely idea with *BBC Online* magazine. We issued a Boxing Day challenge for bored internet surfers to write a Christmas present thank-you letter. The test was to create two letters using the same words but to completely change the meaning and sentiment of the note by altering the punctuation. The very substance of what editors and proofreaders do all day.

To make it easier to grasp, we provided an example in the press release, the BBC published it – then we left the post-festival revellers to have a go.

Several hundred writers rose to the occasion, and both the BBC and my client were delighted at the response and subsequent media coverage. Here is the winning entry, submitted by Dr Maureen McIver, a Reader in Applied Mathematics at Loughborough University:

Happy New Year Richard my dearest husband,

And I would like to thank you for the beautiful painting. It is so unusual! For a man to buy such a thoughtful gift while on a working trip – what can I say?

I went to the Christmas sales with Kathy, and we also went to the pantomime with Barbara. At college it is quiet, with many staff away skiing. There is a lot to do before your return.

I recommend that you try and see the new release of that film from Russia.

With love,

Natasha.

… and by changing the punctuation….

Happy New Year Richard,

My dearest husband and I would like to thank you for the beautiful painting. It is so unusual for a man to buy such a thoughtful gift.

While on a working trip (what can I say?!) I went to the Christmas sales with Kathy, and we also went to the pantomime! With Barbara at college, it is quiet. With many staff away skiing, there is a lot to do.

Before you return, I recommend that you try and see the new release of that film, "From Russia with love".

Natasha

Spot-on, Dr McIver. The competition was also a triumph for those of us who still campaign for the correct use of the apostrophe – and against the overuse of the exclamation mark!!

Apply the same creativity to your PR and you'll get noticed.

Curiosity

Facts are crucial components on which to build your PR work. If you are doing your own PR and have a small team around you, identify the naturally inquisitive individual who enjoys surfing the net for information, solving puzzles, and is hooked on Sudoku Extreme. If nobody on your team fits that bill, consider employing a bright graduate or student on a short placement and assigning research tasks to them. There are plenty of colleges and universities that run internships and placements, especially for students needing a year in industry or postgraduate experience.

Writing and editing

Some are born writers; others learn the basic rules of grammar and punctuation and then work hard on their style. Whatever your level on the ladder of literary genius, when it comes to press releases, imagine you are writing for 12-year-olds. This means short sentences, simple words, and basic facts in no more than 500 words.

Expert articles will take a little more practice and patience. Rule one is to read your target publications and then copy their style and approach. Ask questions of the editor so you get the brief right and give yourself plenty of time.

Edit your work. When I edit articles sent to me for publication, I nip through, deleting or shortening sentences without losing meaning. When I show others how this can be achieved, they are amazed at how simple it is. Test yourself by writing 250 words on why you want to grow your business. Then edit it back to 100 words whilst retaining the key points. Practise this technique as often as you can.

I may be a bit old school, but for me, the use of correct spelling and accurate grammar in written communication is part of image-building. If you submit badly written text, an editor may decide not to run your story at all. And if you do sneak past an editor, what message does a poorly written piece say about your business? At the very least use your spellchecker. Decide whether the UK or US form for certain words is appropriate. Realise or realize? Different from or different to? (In both cases, the UK usage is first.)

If you want to look deeper into the fascinating subject of the written word, take a look at the books I recommend in the Further Reading appendix.

Confident communication
If you are going to open your business to public scrutiny, you need to be confident in yourself and your business. Many people tell me how at first they felt awkward talking or even writing about themselves. The best remedy for this is practice. Over time, you'll develop your own personal style in telling your news. Being able to talk about yourself to an editor, or to speak in front of an audience, will require inner confidence. Most of us go through life much like the swan, calmly gliding over the water whilst madly paddling beneath the surface. Do yourself a favour and make time to plan and then practise. Nothing beats calming nerves than saying to yourself, "I am ready. I can do this."

Flexibility
With the best will in the world, PR plans rarely go to plan. There are far too many variables in campaigns to be sure that each will align perfectly, and you get the outcome you want. Alex at The Bottle Top found that her choice of sponsorship was off target, but she worked out why and will make different decisions next time.

Accept that you will need to adapt as circumstances beyond your immediate control require a new approach. If you are running your own business, especially in 2021, you'll know what that feels and looks like already.

Relationship building

To be effective in your PR you'll need to adopt the long-haul view of relationship building. Lindhurst Engineering deals with some customers every week, while only hearing from others every 10 years or so when a major project emerges. That's quite a long time for Lindhurst to stay in the corporate memory.

Being good at relationships doesn't mean you have to be a natural extrovert. In my experience, extroverts don't necessarily make the best listeners. On the contrary, if you are good at one-to-one conversation, ask questions, and listen to the answers, then you'll go far. This is as true when getting to know editors and journalists as it is when meeting potential clients. Put them and their needs first and you'll win their respect long-term.

Honesty

I shouldn't need to include this, should I? If you find yourself tempted to embellish the facts, and massage the figures, stop. Public relations is all about building trust with your 'publics'. An honest approach to business and to handling tricky situations should they arise will always win the day.

Tenacity

PR is a marathon, not a sprint. So, you'll need plenty of tenacity. I find this quote from Tim Waterstone, founder of the Waterstones bookshop chain, inspiring: *"Tenacity is everything. Show tenacity, allied to courage and absolute clarity of vision, and you'll win the day, even if it proves to be one heck of a journey before you get there."*

Enjoy the ride. Now it's over to you to plan your very own PR campaign.

Beermat PR Lesson #8
Hone and practise those PR skills

13. Your PR Campaign

Get researching

First step. Flip back to the beginning of this book and, unless you have already made copious notes, remind yourself of the early building blocks. Pain, Premise, Proof. Remember how the TEA REX company has built PR into the very fabric of its brand values and product design.

Next, move into identifying your audiences and what you want to say to them. Your actual and potential customers are probably your most important targets. Alpkit knows exactly who will buy their high-performance outdoor clothing and products, and the narrower circle of their true fans, the Alpkit community, and their 'Ambassadors' who love to get along to their events. But don't overlook other audiences, such as suppliers, employees, and influencers.

Look at your competition and its media presence. What messages are they sending? How do they do this? Via what media? How often do they achieve coverage, and in what forms? More generally, look around at how other companies of all kinds are achieving public awareness. Two questions I ask clients:

- Whose PR activity do you admire most?

- Why does it seem so effective?

What do people know about you now? For the start-up, the answer is probably "nothing at all". If so, fine, you have a nice clean reputational slate. For the fast-growing business, it's a sad fact that entrepreneurs and owner-managers often reckon they know how they are currently perceived by others but are wrong. They have usually come to their conclusions without any hard evidence.

So, get some hard evidence to work with:

- *Run a survey.* Try talking to your customers. Begin by gathering some basic sales data to map their purchasing behaviours. Then use an online tool, like Survey Monkey, to gather ratings for services across a set range, usually 1–10. Finally, a survey should leave a box for comment. These comments can be very enlightening, though not always what you want to hear. Just think about how TripAdvisor has transformed our interaction with the tourism and entertainment industry.

    Professional surveys can be expensive – you might be looking at several thousand pounds from a specialist agency – but for the fast-growing business, this could be a wise investment. If you can't afford this, devise your own questionnaire. Next time you're in town, don't dodge the man with the smile and the clipboard: take part, watch how the interview is conducted and the questions crafted, then adapt for your own purposes.

- *Your company records.* Every day your staff will gather valuable market research information in the form of sales reports, complaints, website comments, etc. Gather this valuable internal information, discuss its relevance with colleagues, and identify key points, good and bad.

- *Existing media coverage.* Take a look at previous news reports about your firm. Were they informative, favourable, critical, or sympathetic? Are you being ignored in favour of your rivals? How are they being covered?

- *Employee attitudes.* These are important, because motivated, positive staff act as ambassadors for the company, while miserable, demotivated staff do the opposite. Check indicators such as staff turnover – but most important of all, talk to your people and ask them what they think. No amount of PR will cover a company whose employees are telling the world it's awful.

Though a one-off survey is useful, remember to keep asking. Watch social media messages for any trends. Most useful of all, as your company grows, get your staff to ask. I was recently chatting with a good friend Lizzie Mack who is the Kitchen Manager of Stray's Coffee. They have shops in Newark, Oakham, and Stamford. Lizzie has trained her staff to get into a conversation with customers as they are serving. She rewards her staff who are good at this because the company and customers benefit from feedback.

If you're a fast-growing business, you may move up to employing a PR agency.

I say more about appointing a PR agency later.

Agree your campaign objectives
Having established your general strategy, become more aware of how others see you, looked around at others' PR, and (if you're large enough) sorted out a budget, it's time to sit down and plan your PR campaign in more detail. The first step is to decide what you want to achieve. Our old friend 'SMART' is applicable here: make your goals:

- Specific
- Measurable – include numerical targets where possible
- Achievable – don't overstretch resources
- Relevant – to overall company goals
- Timed – set timescales

Now define the possible outcomes:
- A rise in call traffic.
- Increase in the number of visitors to your site.
- Increase in foot traffic (to events, bricks, and mortar stores, etc).
- Increase in conversions (generated by yourself and can include anything from a form-filling exercise on your site to speaking on live chat).
- The number of annual award nominations.
- Increase in social media followers and/or sharers.

Best of all are revenue-based outcomes (PR is, in the end, only a means to those ends). So…
- Increase in revenue in a specific item or range.
- More donations if you are a charity.
- …. and sales.

Set a budget

If you are a start-up working on a tight budget, you'll be using your own time for PR. I suggest three or four hours per week should allow you to make some good progress.

My tip for anyone in this situation is to get a PR coach. This person will set you some simple tasks to get your PR going and, more generally, discuss ideas with you. It's one of the services I offer, and I find two or three hours a month by phone or email with a client is enough to help them to get basic PR tasks completed and to discuss the outcomes. This is probably the most flexible and cost-effective PR solution for the newer firm: you're getting the input of a PR expert whilst learning the art of business and personal promotion. And it's not costing you a fortune. Just remember to allocate a cost to your time.

If you decide to outsource your PR to a freelancer who will work for you on a part-time basis, your costs will rise. Day rates vary greatly: anywhere between £350 and £850. Few agencies would consider taking on a new client for under £10,000 a year, and you are more likely to be looking at annual fees of £15,000 to £20,000 for a small company contract. This buys you the agency's ability to plan and research your PR needs, manage regular news distribution, and monitor how it is all going.

Don't expect survey work or media tracking. This is usually an additional charge and is provided by a specialist coverage-tracking agency scanning UK print, online, and broadcast media for keywords. If you do use such a service, be very specific with the search terms you give them. You don't want someone else's coverage or generic sector pieces.

Plan the campaign

Here's the time to get creative. I like using Mind Mapping© but you could just as easily use sticky notes against a wall to dump all the campaign ideas that come into your head. Another free tool is Google Jamboard, which enables you to create a virtual post-it board. There's also a free tool called Miro which has three editable boards. Colleagues, clients, or market research focus groups can vote on each board to tell you which one is their favourite.

Let's look at an example together.

Imagine you are running a public awareness campaign, driven by the concern that too many young carers struggle to eat a healthy diet. It's most likely a promotional activity by a charity giving support to carers.

Start your mind map by focusing on the target audience. Consider the problems they face and possible solutions. This will then begin to spark ideas. Write them all down. If I'm scribbling on a plain sheet of paper, or throwing sticky notes at the wall, I find using colours, images and pictures will get creative juices flowing.

The example here is just the beginning of a download of thoughts; later some will be discarded, but don't cut anything out until you have exhausted all possible ideas for your PR campaign. It's important not to restrict yourself or worry that something might be a bad idea. At this stage, there is no such thing as a bad idea.

When you feel you have exhausted all possibilities, leave the mind map for a few hours, then return to it with a fresh pair of eyes.

Having established various possible PR-able options, weed out the ones that are impracticable or, on reflection, don't seem appropriate. Select those that you feel will generate the best results. Apply sensible targets for them – then go out and make it happen, using all the techniques I have described in this book.

Measuring success
At the same time, keep monitoring how your PR is working. You can't beat the most direct question to anyone getting in touch with the company for the first time: "And how did you get to hear of us?"

Don't expect 100 per cent reliability in the answers, but you'll be able to spot trends. Keep asking customers and potential customers if they have seen any media coverage.

Whatever you do, don't just rely on gut feel when measuring. "We got some media coverage, and I'm sure this has contributed something to our success, though of course, I can't tell how much," isn't good enough.

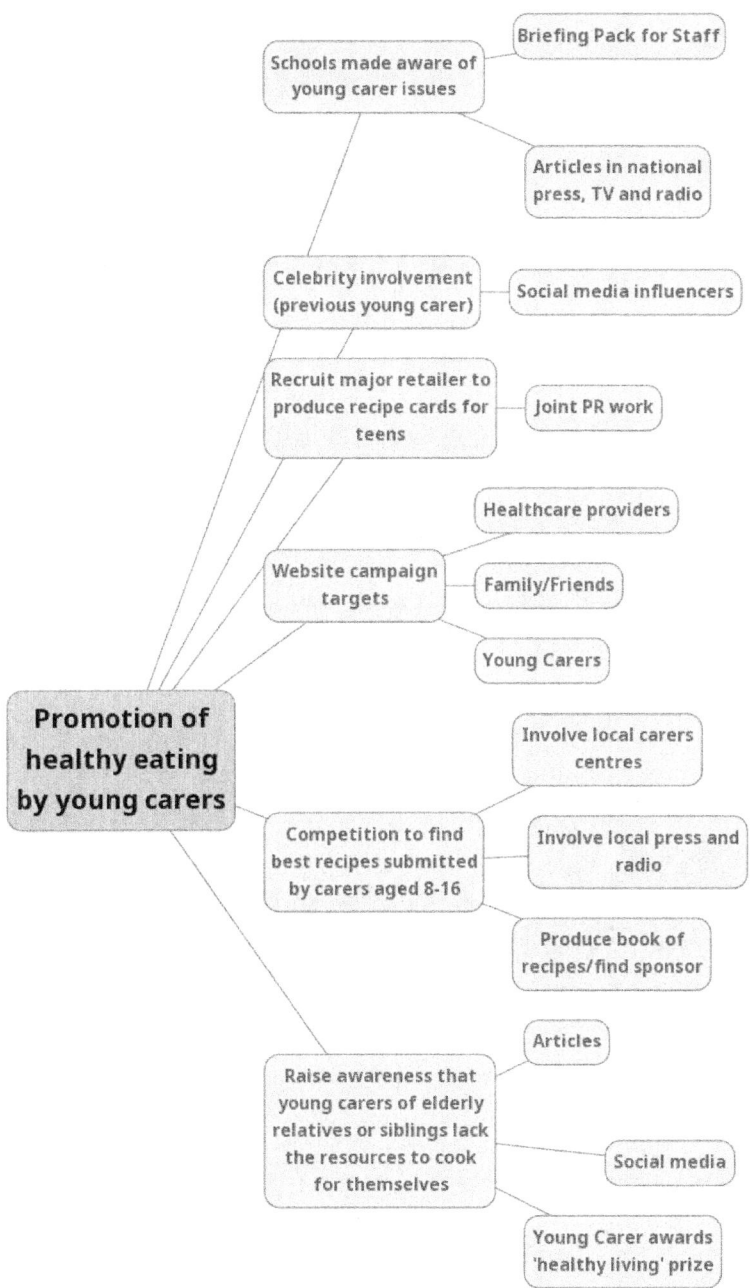

14. Crisis Management

Billionaire investor and philanthropist Warren Buffett provided the quote that resonates in the hearts and minds of every PR professional.

> *"It takes 20 years to build a reputation and five minutes to ruin it. If you think about that, you'll do things differently."*

Buffett's words are a salutary reminder to guard what we do and say.

We all have a reputation. It probably started to form early on, at school: I trust you were the one who shared your last sweet and not the one who threw the punches. Heading into our careers, we developed our characteristics, skills, and little quirky habits. "She has a reputation for being a bit…" "He has a reputation for having a…" It's just part of being human, but your reputation will affect the way others behave around you.

The Chartered Institute for Public Relations puts it more formally:

> *"Reputation is the result of what you do, what you say, and what others say about you. Reputation affects people's behaviour. Behaviour is 'reality' – sales, investment, political or campaign votes, and funding."*

This might seem a little daunting and make you wonder why you ever decided to lift your head above the parapet in the form of a new business. Will it get shot off at the slightest hint of a poor decision, or small issue, or client moan?

It will certainly get shot *at*. As an entrepreneur, freelancer, or small business owner you will learn to take this in your stride, but it's how you deal with it that makes all the difference to being respected or rejected.

Sometimes, your business can be thrown into a position that requires immediate action in the face of negativity, or difficult questions that need answering. We're living in a world where "no comment" is not acceptable, nor is burying your head deep into the sand in the hope that this horrible situation will miraculously disappear. Many smaller organisations get caught up in emergencies that can have an impact on their reputation. Much will depend on whether the crisis is of their own making or caused by a third party, and then on how they handle the response.

Crises can take several forms:

- **Financial.** Cash flow issues and redundancies will always be hot topics for business journalists.
- **Your people.** Your staff are your business and if a member is involved in something they shouldn't be, you and your business will also be in the spotlight.
- **Technological.** A lot of data, including customer details, are stored online. Hackings and technology failure can happen and often lead to serious reputational damage.
- **Organisational.** Accidents on site, complaints and general negligence always require swift action to avoid them being escalated and getting out of hand.
- **A dud new product.** Maybe your business introduces a new product or service which receives a barrage of customer complaints. The Coca-Cola Company's 'New Coke' remains the classic example.
- **Natural.** We're not immune to natural disasters. Floods, fire, snow, and ice are just a few environmental hazards that by their nature happen quickly and can cause havoc. It is how you deal with the situation that can make or break a reputation. For example, if flood waters have entered your premises and your stored chemicals then leach into the water system, you will have some questions to answer.

- **Unforeseen.** The COVID-19 pandemic is a global extreme example of an unforeseen event. Do you react in a sensitive way to staff worried about their jobs, or do you simply tell them they can leave and go and work for a major supermarket (as one high-profile business owner did)?

When such ugly situations arise, the last thing you want to be doing is scrambling around and panicking. If you have staff, your actions and feelings can cause unrest and tension.

My advice is to plan for a worst-case scenario. Major corporations have risk assessment and crisis plans built into the very fabric of their sustainability strategy. On a slightly smaller, but no less important, scale, you should do the same. The purpose of your plan is to minimise the damage, not only to people and the physical surroundings but also to your reputation.

Once you have alarmed yourself by listing the things that could possibly go wrong, calm yourself by creating an issues-handling plan. Yes, call them issues, not crises. They will appear slightly more manageable. The section in your plan on Communications will be the biggest and should start with designating a senior person to coordinate information gathering and sharing.

Everyone in your organisation, from the company chairman through to the receptionist, should be given a role and be briefed on that role should an issue arise.

It's all about remaining in control of the situation and putting your well-honed plan into action. This will make dealing with the emergency services, trade unions, the public, and the media so much easier.

Here are a few tips:

- **Do not say "no comment"**. This instantly implies that you have something to hide or that you are just not prepared or on top of the situation.
- **Appoint your spokesperson**. Make sure you or a relevant senior member of your team is attributing their name to any statement to ensure the words carry authority.
- **Be honest.** Your customers want to know how you're going to respond and fix the issue.
- **Be proactive**. Don't shy away from the situation, even if you don't necessarily have an answer yet. If a journalist is asking a question, remain in touch, and work with them. Journalists remember those who are helpful and are more likely to help you out in return.
- **Communication is key**. Make sure the rest of your staff and stakeholders are aware of the situation to stop the spread of any unnecessary gossip.
- **Keep it simple**. Don't over-complicate a situation or use jargon that people don't understand. Keep it simple. Answer the question.

You might be tempted to see the media as the most hostile element when trouble looms. But don't. Local media play an important role in getting immediate information to the public, especially where personal safety is at stake. Don't leave it to the fire and rescue service or the police to act as your spokespeople. That's not their role. Work together to provide the facts as best you can, and to update these facts as an incident unfolds. The media will expect this, and they will thank you for your willingness to cooperate.

Most issues, I truly hope, won't involve you in a major public security incident. We are more familiar with the company having to close a factory, or a restaurant found to have cockroaches in the kitchens. I can't imagine any of my readers being in any way irresponsible or running a dubious venture. However, like the Biblical parable of the Wise and Foolish Virgins, the wise entrepreneur is well-prepared.

Not only will you have annually updated your Issues Handling plan, but you will also have taken some training in the unlikely event you need it. You will most likely be the spokesperson for media interviews, but you could pay someone like Dan Baker, of PLC Media, to speak on your behalf. We met Dan earlier and I have another hypothetical question for him.

Question: A member of staff has gone to the local paper about my company and our current financial difficulties. They don't think I'm handling things well and have said they believe around 20 staff will be made redundant. That's quite a lot for a small town. The news desk wants to interview me so what's the best way to defend my reputation and be truthful at the same time?

Answer: "The most important thing is to be honest. If you're going to have to lay off staff, then say that. Crucially, you'll have already talked to the staff – this is where it is so important that internal and external communications tie in with each other. But if you've got to impart bad news, think of it as showing strong leadership by fronting up to it in an interview. Obviously, a smile isn't appropriate, but don't look too anxious or upset or it looks like you've got no control over the situation. Show warmth, show empathy, and show reassurance through the language you use, through the simplicity of the message, through the performance.

If you can see the storm clouds gathering on a story like this, consider some media training: getting it right will leave people feeling that you did the best you could, getting it wrong will make it look like you simply don't care. And there are far, far too many examples of the latter out there right now."

Many books, articles and blogs have been written on crisis communications and there is plenty of advice available from professionals like Dan.

When the metaphorical fire is extinguished, take time to breathe a heavy sigh of relief. You'll have earned it. But don't rest on your laurels. Evaluate. If something went wrong, can it be fixed to avoid a repeat? Who knows, maybe your next crisis exposes a flaw you didn't know your business had and allows you to sort the situation before it gets even bigger.

> **Beermat PR lesson #9**
> *Plan for success, but anticipate the occasional crisis*

15. Internal PR

Ok, so you have a good grasp of how to deal with difficult external situations. You're doing what it takes to look after your customers, your clients, and your stakeholders. Excellent – but have you thought about your staff? Do they like working for you? Do they like their job? Do they feel supported?

A business' reputation starts with its people. Word of mouth remains important even in this digitally saturated world. What are your colleagues saying about the company away from the office to their nearest and dearest? In turn, what are they saying to their friends? Like a wildfire, bad feelings and sentiment soon spread.

One of the biggest reasons a colleague leaves a business is due to poor communications. It can affect productivity, culture, leadership, and the cost of doing business.

Your biggest asset is the staff who work for you. Poor communication leads to bad feelings and an environment of distrust and confusion. By putting together an effective internal communications plan you are providing the following:

- Transparency to keep your colleagues informed on all facets of the business.
- A two-way approach where no one feels voiceless.
- A culture that allows everyone to feel part of something.
- A reason to engage and give their best.
- A comfortable channel for colleagues to provide feedback, debate, and discussion.

What does an engaging internal communications strategy look like?
No matter how big your business is now or in the future, there are still several tried and tested methods that will help you begin to build the culture you want for your business and the people helping you drive it forward. Some of the following tips may not apply to you or where your business is at right now, but they may come in handy in the future.

Make the most of technology
Emails are great for communicating professionally with your clients and stakeholders, but tools such as Slack and Microsoft Teams are internal messaging tools with a proven track record of producing collaboration and communication between colleagues.

Internal newsletters
Think about introducing a newsletter to keep the latest nuggets about the business in front of the staff. Keep the content lively by inviting colleagues to contribute. Make it fun, relevant, and engaging by including quizzes, Q&As, and photos.

Give your people a reason to open it. Weave into the lighter items a few company updates. This is a quick and simple way to paint a picture of how things are going. Make it easy for your team to comment and ask questions.

Encourage staff social media use
We spoke in-depth about how you can use your social media for good, but wouldn't it be great if your staff and colleagues were also sharing that content, too?

Work with your people to turn them into micro social influencers and invite them to post positive news about your business and the work you are all doing.

Open-door policy

Above everything else, your staff want to know they can come to you if they have a problem or if they have something positive to share. Such an approach can avert a potential crisis if a staff member feels able to approach you with an issue rather than tackle it themselves or go to the local press

---

Beermat PR Lesson #10

Look after your staff and they'll look after your reputation

16. Choosing a PR Consultancy

This book has largely assumed that you are in the very early stages of your start-up venture. Perhaps you are already working freelance or want to grow your small business. You are on a tight budget, and you need to do the PR work yourself.

However, if you have reached a critical point in your business journey where outsourcing to PR experts makes more sense, then this section is for you.

Having read this book, and put some of its advice into action, you will have absorbed something of the PR mindset. This will prepare you well for your search for the right PR firm.

Search or recommendation?

You can search for an agency by sector or location. Do you need a service with a nationwide sector specialism, such as pharmaceuticals, or one that specialises in having a solid knowledge of (and, more important, contacts in) media in your region? The answer depends, of course, on how your market or potential market is segmented.

Either way, don't just pick an agency at random. Ask around for recommendations. If you admire the coverage a company is getting, find out who manages their PR. They might be able to do the work for you too if there is no conflict of interest in representing both firms.

The professional bodies, PRCA and CIPR mentioned in Chapter One, provide a search facility that will put you in touch with their members according to location or specialism – it's a start but don't rely solely on this.

Richard Tyler, the editor of The Times Enterprise Network, says: "If you do hire a PR firm, make sure they specialise in promoting small businesses. Some larger PR firms simply give their small business clients to more junior staff to cut their teeth. Nothing guarantees zero press coverage better than a PR person who neither understands the story nor smaller businesses more broadly."

Ouch. Brutal, but worth remembering when you start to outsource your publicity work.

The PR brief

Draw up a shortlist, meet a few agencies on an informal basis, and then invite two or three to tender for your work. A PR professional can only do this according to a clear campaign brief. The brief should contain the following:

- A summary of your company and its key activities.
- A description of your marketing objectives.
- An indication of any issues or barriers facing you.
- Details about the main target audiences and the results of any research into them.
- A description of your current communications methods and their effectiveness.
- What you want to achieve from PR.
- How you will measure the success of the PR activity.
- Who will oversee managing the activity on behalf of the firm?
- An indication of budget.

Selection criteria for a PR agency

Based on the written submissions, choose those you want to interview. Try to gauge their skills in the following:
- Ability to communicate
- Ability to organise

- Ability to get on with people
- Personal integrity
- Imagination
- Willingness to learn
- Quality of media contacts. This is the most important thing. You should expect the agency to show you a sample of coverage they have gained in your sector. Ask them to talk through a campaign they have worked on; this way you will be able to judge how they use their media contacts to best effect.
- Contacts need not be just media contacts. Agencies that specialise in a particular industry should have contacts with influencers in that sector and be able to connect you with potential strategic partners, or, for charities, potential sponsors. They should also be able to tell you a bit about your competition.

If your business is conducted largely online, you should look for an agency with strong web and social media expertise. You would expect such an agency to have a good media presence but also rank well on Google for key search terms. So, check out the following:

- Do they rank high on Google for marketing agencies in the area?
- Does this agency have case studies that show they have achieved an increase in brand awareness/search rankings through PR?
- Do they have experience in your sector?
- Do you get along with the staff? Ideally, you'd want to go to the pub with someone from the agency – likeability is essential!

Having gone through written and interview procedures, get some references.

Then decide.

What questions to expect from a PR Agency.

We enlisted the help of Hallam's client services team to give you an insight into the type of questions you and your business should expect if you were to approach an agency like Hallam.

Question: When an enquiry comes through from a business, what are the first questions you ask?

Answer: Essentially, we get a feel for what the client is trying to achieve, and how well suited we may be to help them, rather than just what services they want. Ideally, this is done through an initial phone call when we will cover:

- **Your company** – we build a profile of the business, how it operates, the number of staff, its revenue, what markets it serves, and who its competitors are.
- **What you want to achieve** – we want to find out the primary objectives of the business, which will help to focus the proposal we put together.
- **What is required** – how you think we can help you and how you came to that decision.
- **What resources your business already has in place** – we need to know whether you already have in-house experts we can work with or whether we will be delivering all the work, or even simply providing training.
- **What budget you are working with** – an indication of budget, either for marketing overall or for agency spend.
- **Who the decision-makers are in the business** – we want to be speaking with the people making the decisions as well as the team we would be working with?

Those initial conversations allow us to go away and put together a proposal. For example, if a business comes to us and says they want to triple their revenue over the next five years, that's great. That's a strategic objective and one we can focus our energy on. Not all businesses can be that specific, but that's OK, too. By talking, it quickly becomes apparent what is important and what isn't.

Question: You mention the budget. Is it imperative that a business owner or marketing manager approaches an agency and knows exactly what they are looking to spend?

Answer: It is important that a business either knows what budget they have for the work or, if there isn't a specific budget, what they are prepared to invest once they have discussed the options with us.

Question: Should a business approach these initial meetings with an open mind because their digital marketing goals might not be realistic?

Answer: Definitely. The more open a business is to suggestions on solutions for their goals, the better. We get several businesses that will come to us firmly believing they need to improve x or y, but in fact, a different solution may provide better results. Solutions vary and by bringing together our different experts we are better able to find the best route forward.

Question: How do we know which type of agency to approach? Do we go with a strategic full-service agency, or to a smaller independent specialist, or even a smaller integrated agency?

Answer: There are a lot of choices, and you want to get it right. Rather than just approach one agency, businesses will often target several and that is where the tender pitch comes in. Much like when you are buying a house, you just get a feeling. You will know which agency is the best for you from the way they get to know your business and what you value. Importantly, they will also demonstrate their expertise.

Working together

Whoever you choose, the chances are you will work together for a trial period if you appoint them on a retainer basis. Six months will allow you to gauge their rate of progress and eagerness to work with you – but don't expect to have gained significant coverage by then. Be reasonable, unless it is obvious that the level of outputs in terms of ideas, news, or articles is inadequate. Remember that an agency is as reliant on your firm's responsiveness to requests and ability to generate PR-able activity as you are on them to make something happen!

Andrew Walker of TEA REX adds that your own firm should also pitch well if you want a good agency to decide to work for you. It's a two-way selection process.

Beermat PR Lesson #11
Your PR agency is one of the team.
Trust them. Help them.

17. PR in Action

So, there you have it. The entrepreneur's guide to PR and how it works. A smorgasbord of activity you can try out as your new venture takes off. You've heard enough from me, Tom, and Rebecca. Now we want to leave it to the entrepreneurs to share some final advice before we release you to go and make some noise.

What should anyone new to PR do before they start any promotional campaign?

Nadine Cooper, Tuneless Choir: "Really develop and understand what makes you and your venture unique. Then write consistently about it. Get a library of decent photos and videos together too."

Alex Preston, The Bottle Top: "Think about the message but also the audience. Having a brilliantly crafted PR piece is one thing but it can be a waste of time and finances if it is delivered to the wrong audience. Understanding your core customer base and what it is you wish to gain from the PR campaign is where the value lies."

David Hanney, Alpkit: "Be clear. Know what you want to say and why you want to say it."

Andrew Walker, TEA REX: "Try to have everything in place first. We entered the Great Taste Awards probably sooner than we should have by sending in a few samples made in my kitchen. Next thing we know we are being invited to the BBC Good Food Show attended by 25,000 people, so we had to make 4,000 sachets to take with us. It worked, but not without giving us a few headaches."

Martin Rigley, Lindhurst: "Pick one very clearly defined message you want to get across and stick to this, no matter what PR vehicle you use."

What are the main lessons you have learned from using PR?

Nadine: "It's not actually too difficult if you follow advice. The hardest part is finding a good story and the right angle on it. I was going to say it's not rocket science, but maybe NASA's PR would disagree! It's well worth doing. Some people turn up as customers years after they've read about you in a paper or seen you on TV. And they can be genuinely new contacts, not from your social bubble or friends of existing customers. When you get a piece of coverage then share, share, share on social media! Be sure to tag the journalist as well as the publication – if you are nice about what they've written they'll probably share your comments."

Alex: "That you don't always have to say yes. Turning down PR 'opportunities' that don't quite work or fit your business is not a bad thing. Money and time are precious, so putting them where they will be put to the best use is highly important. Also, there *is* such a thing as bad PR. Despite what people say, bad press can be highly damaging to a business so being careful about who you work with and ensuring they align with you and your ethos is really important."

Andrew: "We don't separate PR from the brand. Instead, the PR opportunities are built into TEA REX. Whether we are talking to buyers, exhibition visitors, or the media, what we have to offer raises a smile."

Martin: "You are not bragging when you want to tell the world about the great work you do. Although reporters will try to get you to tell the story they want, stick to your message. People want to hear good news stories, especially if it's about a success in their area or line of work."

What would you do differently if you were starting now?

Nadine: "More and more news coverage and PR opportunities are online. It's a 24/7 news cycle and journalists are more stretched. I'm not quite sure what I could do differently but there's pressure to do more personal stories – it seems the more dramatic the better."

Alex: "We wouldn't change much, as it has all been a valuable lesson. However, I think I would invest more in PR: having a regular line of contact with our local community is the single most important thing that keeps us in business, particularly trading through a pandemic. I think I heard somewhere that the magic number is 15 points of contact; if I had realised how powerful PR could be, I would have definitely done more of it and made sure I had done it more effectively by asking for help and advice from the experts."

David: "I would have started out sooner. I worked for other people too long!"

Martin: "I wish I had realised the power of PR earlier than I have done, having spent the first 16 years of my business career in radio silence. It's not until we started to get some press recognition 10 years ago that we recognised it can bring great benefits for a business in terms of standing in the community and the wider business world.

"In 1990 we manufactured 22 bespoke pieces of equipment to produce pre-stressed concrete railway sleepers and never really told anyone. Thirty years later the equipment was still functioning and had produced over eight million sleepers for the UK rail infrastructure. We had the opportunity to be recognised globally for our expertise in this field and we missed it."

Any last-minute advice?

Alex: "Take your time and reach out for help if you feel you need assistance. Have confidence in yourself and your business. Every business has a story to tell and something worth shouting about."

Beermat PR Lesson #12
Tell your story to whoever will listen

---

18. And finally…

If like me, you enjoy running your business and want even more people to know about what you do, you will love PR. If this book has inspired you to tackle the PR work yourself, great. Please let us know how you get on via www.pronabeermat.co.uk. If, however, you would rather buy the services of a PR or digital agency and leave the work to them, at least you will be able to appoint the person with the right skills. You'll probably be able to spot whether your funds are being well spent too.

A core tenet of Beermat is that 'business is about people', so putting public relations at the heart of your business is a fundamental Beermat lesson. Failure to do so will mean you miss out on some amazing reputation-building opportunities and allow your competition to take all the limelight. Don't do this!

So, I challenge you to set yourself a few PR-related goals for the coming months based on the guidance in this book.

First, a reminder of the #12 Beermat PR Lessons.

Beermat PR Lesson #1
PR is for me and my new venture

Beermat PR lesson #2
My new venture are I are both unique

Beermat PR lesson #3
Target, target, target.

Beermat PR Lesson #4
News should be topical and timely

Beermat PR Lesson #5
Think like a journalist

Beermat PR Lesson #6
Blow your own trumpet –
but make sure it's pleasant for the listener

Beermat PR Lesson #7
Get digitally savvy

Beermat PR Lesson #8
Hone and practise those PR skills

Beermat PR lesson #9
Plan for success, but anticipate the occasional crisis

Beermat PR Lesson #10
Look after your staff and they'll look after your reputation

Beermat PR Lesson #11
Your PR agency is one of the team. Trust them. Help them.

Beermat PR Lesson #12
Tell your story to whoever will listen

Now set aside time to put Beermat PR wisdom into action.

- Draw your PR campaign using a mind map, spider diagram, or sticky notes on the wall. Simply jot down ideas as they emerge.
- Build a database of the editors and writers who cover your sector. Say hello to them.
- Aim to get two articles published in your trade press. Long reads are still popular.
- Recruit a student on placement to design and carry out a simple communications audit.
- Research and enter at least one trade award. I know your winning speech will knock 'em dead.
- Write a crisis-handling plan. I hope you never need it.
- Keep a diary of your business journey. It will provide useful content should a journalist need your insights. You'll eventually be able to read it to your grandchildren and make them smile.

Do tell us how your PR activity is going: the successes as well as the frustrations.

You can find us on Twitter @louisethird, @tbestwick93, @mikesouthon and @chriswestwriter, and all our profiles on LinkedIn.

Bookmark pronabeermat.co.uk where we will post blogs, podcasts, and videos to keep the Beermat PR conversation running.

Join us and inspire others to get writing, celebrating, and shouting about the ups and downs of being your own boss, and using PR to make some noise.

Special thanks to…

Beermat editor-in-chief Chris West, and author and entrepreneur Mike Southon who placed their trust in me to write, and re-write, this Beermat guide to public relations. I'm so glad I plucked up the courage to say hello all those years ago.

Hallam for lending me digital marketing and PR experts Tom Bestwick and Rebecca Peel, and to Alun Davies for a fabulous cover design. They have kept to deadlines, kept me motivated and been a pleasure to work with.

Entrepreneurs Andrew Walker, Nadine Cooper, Alex Preston, David Hanney, Martin Rigley, Cheryl Stretton and Rory Thorpe who willingly answered my questions to bring life and colour to the book.

Journalists Tom Witherow, Maisha Frost, Richard Tyler, and Natalie Fahy. Where would we be without independent, editorial scrutiny of all our gushing press releases and announcements? Consuming fake news, I guess. So, let's call for a National Journalist Appreciation Day and do our bit to challenge misinformation and disinformation.

Technical experts Jack Delaney for his video & film production advice, author and publisher Ladey Adey, and Dan Baker whose crisis handling and media training provide a 'port in a storm' if things go wrong.

Proofreader and guardian of the correct use of punctuation, Nicola Ball. I promise never to hyphenate incorrectly or exclaim without good reason.

Finally, you the reader for believing in the Beermat way of doing business, buying the book, reading it, and recommending it to others. Please stay in touch on pronabeermat.co.uk.

Contacts

louisethird.com	Louise Third PR Consultancy
pronabeermat.co.uk	Connect, order, and learn from the dedicated book website
hallam.co.uk	Hallam, Digital Agency
mikesouthon.com	Home of all things 'Beermat'
chriswest.info	Professional writer (and editor of this book)
plcmedia.com	Dan Baker, PLC Media
simply-thrilled.com	Jack Delaney's video firm
ladeyadey.com	Ladey Adey, author and publisher
prca.org.uk	The Public Relations and Communications Association
cipr.co.uk	The Chartered Institute of Public Relations

Our entrepreneurs

And here are some of the companies you've read about…

tunelesschoir.com	The Tuneless Choir
thebottletopnotts.co.uk	The Bottle Top
alpkit.com	Alpkit
tearex.co.uk	TEA REX Fruit Infusions
ruddyfine.co.uk	The Ruddy Fine Distillery Ltd
lindhurstengineering.co.uk	Lindhurst Engineering

Useful podcasts

Marketing Over a Coffee
Social Media Marketing Podcast

Start-ups For the Rest of Us
The Hustle and Flowchart Podcast
Online Marketing Made Easy
Perpetual Traffic
The Next 100 Days
The Humans Strike Back
Simon Sinek podcast series.

Useful sites

Alliance of Independent Authors	allianceindependentauthors.org
United Ghost-writers	unitedghostwriters.co.uk
The Drum	thedrum.com
PR Moment	prmoment.com
PR Week	prweek.com/uk

Further reading

The Beermat Entrepreneur (Third Edition), Mike Southon & Chris West, Pearson 2018

Sales on a Beermat (Second Edition), Mike Southon & Chris West, 2020

Marketing on a Beermat, Chris West, Random House 2008

Small is Beautiful – A study of Economics as if People Mattered (First Edition 1973) E.F. Schumacher, HarperCollins 2010

Perfect Written English, Chris West, Random House 2008

Into the Woods: How stories work and why we tell them, John Yorke, Penguin 2013

Your problem, our story: a management guide to handling emergencies and the media, Philip Algar, Matfield Books 2008

The Copywriter's Handbook, Robert W. Bly, Macmillan Publishers 2020

Year Ahead, The Profile Group, Centaur Media

A modest book about how to make an adequate speech, John-Paul Flintoff, Short Books, 2021

Successful Business Networking Online, Ladey Adey 2021

Printed in Great Britain
by Amazon